The Character
Of God's Workman

The
Character
Of God's Workman

WATCHMAN NEE

Translated from the Chinese

Christian Fellowship Publishers, Inc.
New York

ISBN 0-935008-69-1

Available from the Publishers at:

11515 Allecingie Parkway
Richmond, Virginia 23235

PRINTED IN U.S.A.

TRANSLATOR'S PREFACE

In the work of God, the worker is more important than the work. If God cannot find the right person, He would rather delay His work. Much time and effort will He spend in the training of a workman fit for the Master's use. Basically, the training is more in the area of character than of skill. Only a new creation can serve God. Positionally, "if any man is in Christ, he is a new creation" (2 Cor. 5.17mg.); experientially, old habits will have to be shed and new habits formed through the working of the cross in his life. A few principal characteristics of the life of Christ need to be incorporated in the worker before he is qualified to be a servant of God. Otherwise, God's work will suffer in his hands. It is far better for him not to plunge himself at all into the most sacred work of God.

Seeing the importance of the workman's character in the service of God, Watchman Nee gave a series of messages on this subject to a group of fellow-workers in Kuling in 1948, which was subsequently published in Chinese. A condensed version, in English translation, was published by the Church Book Room, Hong Kong, in 1965, it being the work of the late Miss Elizabeth Fischbacher. It was a work beautifully done and of the highest quality. Sensing, however, the tremendous significance of these messages in relation to God's work and His workmen, a new English translation of the *full* text seems now to be in order. While so doing, the spoken form of these messages has been preserved and only necessary editing done for clarity.

The fundamental features of the character of God's workman given by Watchman Nee are that he: (1) is able to listen, (2) loves all mankind, (3) has a mind to suffer, (4) buffets his body and brings it into subjection, (5) is diligent and not slothful, (6) is restrained in speech, (7) is stable, (8) is not subjective, (9) has a right attitude towards money, and (10) is dealt with on some other important matters.

CONTENTS

1 | Able to Listen

To one who does the work of the Lord, his personal life matters much with respect to his work. What he is in his character, habit and conduct is essential to his being used of God. This is something to which we need to pay close attention. It speaks of the formation of our nature and the cultivation of our habit. It is more than merely having an experience before God, it involves the forming of character. The Lord has to create a new character in us. In many areas of life we need to be exercised before the Lord until there be developed in us new habits. These things have more to do with our outward man for it is there that we are re-created so as to be fit for the Master's use.

Naturally, all this will necessitate the grace and the mercy of God. Nothing is completed on any day. Yet with sufficient light and adequate word from the Lord, all that is of ourselves and which is unfit will be withered and discontinued under the light, while at the same time a new character will be given us in resurrection, through God's mercy. The few qualities which we shall mention hereafter have been drawn from the experiences and understanding of a number of brothers and sisters who have faithfully served God for many years. If any of these fundamental qualities is missing in a worker, the work of God shall surely suffer.

One

The first quality to be mentioned is the ability to listen. One who does the work of the Lord must possess in his personal life the habit of being a good listener. This is not just listening obediently but listening with understanding as well. It is a great need in the personal life of a worker. No one can do good work if he is always talking and never listening. A person whose mouth goes on continually like firecrackers that crack one after another is useless in God's hand. No workman of God can be always talking. For how can he discern the problem of the person he is conversing with if he is speaking all the time. He is absolutely useless in helping people. When a person comes to you wishing to talk, you must learn how to listen before God. As he speaks, you need to be able to decipher three different kinds of words: (1) the words spoken, (2) those unspoken, and (3) those hidden within his spirit.

First, we must be able to hear and understand the words spoken. When someone comes to you, you yourself must be a quiet person whose heart is unperturbed and whose spirit is tranquil. You are like a piece of white blank paper having no prejudice, no subjectiveness and no inclination. Within you there is neither decision nor judgment. You place yourself in God's presence in a state of perfect stillness. As soon as that person opens his mouth and begins to talk, you learn to listen to his words. In quietly listening you are able to know and understand what he is saying.

It is not an easy thing to listen. How much do you really understand when a brother is talking about a certain problem? Sometimes a dozen people, listening to a brother speaking of just one thing, may hear a dozen different things. What you hear is one thing, and what another person hears is another. And hence, there may be dozens of different conclusions drawn. How terrible it is if a truth is to be interpreted in dozens of ways. Therefore, learning to listen is a very necessary and basic discipline. Learning to understand the words spoken by people is a fundamental lesson a worker of God must learn.

When someone comes to you with a heavy burden and pours out his trouble, he expects to receive some help from you. But if you listen wrongly, what will happen? Or if you have not heard his story in the slightest but try to answer him with the thought that has been in your mind for the last two days, what kind of mess will you be creating? Suppose, for example, that a person has had an idea running through his mind during the last two days. He shares the same thought with the healthy as well as the sick, with the joyful as well as the mournful. He cannot simply sit down and listen quietly to what someone in need tells him. Do you think he can help anyone? Obviously not. So when someone is speaking to you, you as a workman of the Lord must listen carefully and try to discover what that person is really saying.

It is a far more difficult task for a workman of God to deal with people's spiritual problems than for a physician to examine his patients for physical problems. This is because a physician is assisted by the tests performed in the laboratory, whereas a worker for God tests everything with himself. A brother or a sister comes to you and talks for half an hour. During this half hour he places all his problems before you. You know nothing about his daily life nor his family situation nor his condition before the Lord. Half an hour is quite a long time; how are you going to help him if you are not a good listener?

All God's workers must develop the ability to sit down, listen and discover the real issue in what they have heard. We who are God's workmen must train ourselves to such a degree that as soon as people begin talking we can begin to know almost immediately where the cause lies. We soon come to have a clear picture in our mind of the situation. And thus shall we know whether we ourselves are competent to handle the case. Sometimes a brother's situation is beyond our ability to help. In that case he should be frankly told. As soon as we hear his words, we know exactly where he stands and where we stand.

Secondly, we must be able to hear and understand the words unspoken. We need to hear before God the words which people have failed to utter. We should discern how much has been said and how much that should have been told but which was not said. To hear the words of the latter is much harder than to hear the words of the former. For whereas in the first case the words are uttered, now we must perceive what are his unuttered words. When people talk, they frequently say only half and leave the other half unsaid. In that event, it is now up to the worker to discern. But should you be undisciplined, you will not be able to hear what has been left unspoken. On the contrary, you will now add in your own ideas which the speaker does not at all have. This betrays something wrong with your own mind. For you bring in by force what he neither conceives in his mind nor utters in his words. You completely misunderstand him.

In order to judge what a person has uttered and what he has not uttered, you must be open before God. Oftentimes people will articulate what is not pertinent but omit what *is* pertinent and therefore important. It depends upon your personal dealings with God as to whether you shall be able to discern if the essential words have been spoken or not. So when a brother comes to speak to you, you need to know clearly what he has *not* uttered as well as what he *has* uttered. And you must also understand what lies behind his unuttered words. Only then will you have confidence before God as to the way of helping him — be it admonition or reproof or whatever. In case you are unclear yourself, you cannot listen — you simply pour out what is in your own mind. But after you have said your last word, you still remain ignorant of his problem; and thus, you have not rendered any help. The fact of the matter is that a poor listener is of very little use to God's work. Unfortunately many seem to be plagued with this disease of an inability to hear either the spoken or the unspoken words. If so, then how can anyone expect them to distribute spiritual food in due season?

Thirdly, we must be able to hear and understand words hidden in man's spirit. Do not only listen to words uttered and unuttered, but also listen to what we would call words in the spirit. As a man opens his mouth and speaks, his innermost spirit is also speaking. As long as he is willing to talk with you, you have the opportunity of touching his spirit; when, however, his mouth is closed, his spirit is shut up within him; and as a consequence, it is not easy to know the words deep inside him. But the moment he opens his mouth, his spirit can begin to come forth. No matter how much he tries to control himself, his spirit will be manifest. Yet whether or not you are able to detect his hidden words in the spirit is dependent largely upon your own spiritual exercise before God. If you have learned, you may know not only the words spoken and unspoken but also the words in the spirit. As he talks you can perceive which few words come from his inner man. And thus you can begin to understand the issue in his spirit as well as the issue in his mind. You are now in a position to deal rightly with that brother. Otherwise, how can you cure his ailment if, after listening for half an hour, you fail to grasp the real issue?

This ability to listen is truly an urgent need for us workers. How sad that not many brothers and sisters are good listeners. You may converse with them for an hour and yet they still do not understand you. Indeed, the ability to listen is far from adequate. If a person cannot understand what man says to him, how can he possibly understand what God is speaking to him? If he cannot hear clearly the words spoken by people who sit close by, how can he hear God who speaks within him from heaven? If he cannot understand man's audible words, how can he understand God's words spoken to his spirit?

What can you say to a brother if you cannot diagnose his spiritual illness and ferret out his problem? Let us not dismiss this as a small matter. For unless we have dealings in this area, we will not become those who can help people, even though we may study the Bible well, preach well and do many other works well. We must not be preachers only, who stand on a platform and speak to people; we must also be those who can deal effectively with them. How can we possibly render assistance to people if we cannot even hear what is being said? May we see the seriousness of this matter.

How much time have you spent before God in learning to listen to what people say? Or have you spent any time on this at all? We should spend time in learning to hear the words spoken, the words unspoken, and also the words in people's spirit. Please understand that a person's mouth and his spirit may not be in one accord. Many people speak one way, and yet their spirits are in a different condition. Nonetheless, a man's mouth is not able to hide his spirit forever. Sooner or later his spirit *will* come forth. And when it does come forth, you will then know exactly where he stands. But without such knowledge, it is rather difficult to help people.

Once upon a time there was an old physician who knew only two drugs: one was castor oil, the other was quinine pills. Regardless who came to him, he either prescribed castor oil or quinine. He used only these two drugs as a panacea for all sicknesses. Similarly, many brothers deal with people in but one or two ways. No matter what the condition of the needy one may be, they always speak the same words of prescription! Such brothers cannot help people. All who are called and used by God must have this one ability: that as soon as a person begins to speak, they know at once or shortly thereafter what that one is saying. Without such an ability, we cannot heal people's spiritual ailments.

Two

How may we hear and understand? *First, we must not be subjective.* Let us be aware that the chief reason for not hearing and understanding other people's words is because of subjectiveness. A subjective person is unable to know what others are saying. In the event you have a preconceived idea or a subjective opinion about a certain thing or person, you will not be able to hear what is said to you. For you are filled with your own thought on the matter or person in question. So firmly is your opinion lodged in you that another's idea cannot have room for consideration.

Returning to our story earlier, regardless the kind of sickness, the doctor of our story has predetermined in his own mind always to prescribe castor oil. So that when confronted by needy people, he only dispenses this prescription. The same is true in the spiritual realm. How can a similarly inclined person possibly hear other people and thus help them? When brothers and sisters come to him, he is in no position to understand and render assistance in their spiritual problems. He has already decided beforehand to say certain words to them; and aside from these words, he has nothing else to say. He may have great confidence in himself, but he has no knowledge of people's difficulties. How, then, can such a person do the work of God?

We must therefore ask the Lord to teach us not to be subjective. Let us say to the Lord, "Lord, cause me to have neither prejudice nor pre-diagnosis when I come into contact with people. Lord, it is not for me to decide what sickness he should have, but cause me to find out what sickness he actually does have." Let us learn before God not to be subjective; let us not be set in our own idea or view. Let us listen carefully. Let us try to touch the hidden cause and discern the real problem.

Second, we must not be absent-minded. Many brothers and sisters are undisciplined in their thought life. Their mind is constantly revolving about with never-ending thoughts. They think of this and think of that; their mind is always full of different ideas. And thus, there is no way for other people's thought, as expressed by their words, to penetrate into their mind. Their brain is never at rest. They are so occupied with their own ideas that they are not able to accept and consider another's thought. In view of this, our mind must be disciplined if we wish to listen to what people say. For when a mind revolves like a wheel, nothing else can get in. When a workman of the Lord listens to another brother or sister, his own mind needs to be stilled. Not only must his will not be subjective; his mind must be still as well. We must learn to think what another thinks and to hear what another says, even to hear the thought within the words. Otherwise, we are of very little usefulness.

Third, we must be sensible to others' feeling. Here is another basic requirement to being a good listener, which is, that as we listen, we need to touch that person's feeling. In order to reach an understanding, we must enter into the other's feeling as we listen to his words. Suppose a person is in deep sorrow and distress, but your own spirit is carefree and jolly. In that case, though you may hear a great deal, nevertheless, nothing registers. This is because your feeling is not in harmony with his feeling. And as a consequence, you cannot comprehend what has happened to him. So that one whose emotion has not been disciplined cannot enter into another's emotion. Unless a person has been dealt with before God, he cannot sing hallelujah at people's joy nor shed tears at their sorrow; and accordingly, he is unable to hear what they say.

How can we enter into the feelings of other people? We must keep our emotion sufficiently neutral. The one who comes before you has his own feeling, and unless your own feeling is neutral you have no ability to feel what he feels. You will be so busily occupied with what you yourself feel that you will be totally unable to know and to enter into how he feels. For the sake of the Lord, we become servants to all the brethren. We give them not only our time and our energy but also our feeling and emotion. This is truly a very weighty matter. In addition to helping people in their affairs, we also enter into their feelings by keeping our own feelings and emotions free. And since our own feelings are free and thus at their disposal, we may easily enter into the feelings of others. This is the meaning of how our Lord Jesus Christ, having been tempted and tested and tried in all things, is able to sympathize with us fully (see Heb. 4.15; cf. 2.18).

What has thus far been said above goes to explain the reason why our emotion must be dealt with. Our affection, having been dealt with, will no longer be self-engrossed; we must not only reserve time and energy for people, we must also reserve our feeling for them. This means we keep neutral our own emotions—be they love or joy or sorrow—whenever we listen to people, so that we may more easily enter into another's emotions. Otherwise, one single feeling of ours may so possess us and fill us that we have no spare room into which to accept another's feeling and thus be able to answer his need.

For one who learns to serve the Lord, the demand of God upon him is very high. He has no time to be joyful for himself, or to be sad for himself. For if he remains joyful or sorrowful, loving or hating in or for himself, he is already so engrossed and filled with his own self that he has no emotional strength left by which to supply the needs of brothers and sisters. Let us therefore understand that God's workman must always hold his emotions in neutrality within himself; otherwise, he will be like a house so full of things that there is no room for anything else.

Many brothers and sisters are unable to do the work of God because they have already exhausted their love.

They cannot undertake anything else. We ought to know that our soulical power is as limited in its capacity as is our physical power and strength. Our affection does have a limit. If we expend more of it in this or that area, we have less or even none remaining for another area.

Is it strange or incorrect to say that he who loves people too much cannot work for the Lord? Yet Jesus said this: "If any man cometh unto me, and hateth not his own father, and mother, and wife, and children, and brethren, and sisters, yea, and his own life also, he cannot be my disciple" (Luke 14.26). Why is this so? Because in loving these people, we have used up all our love. We should love instead the Lord our God—and do so with all our heart, with all our soul, with all our strength and with all our mind. We must take all our love and pour it upon God. It is a good thing if one day we put ourselves to the test and discover how limited we are in our affectional life as well as in other areas of life. We need to know that our capacity is limited. We are like a boat so filled to the full that no more load can be added. As a matter of fact, we do indeed have our limit. In order to enter into the feeling of others, therefore, we need to keep in ready reserve our own feeling, our own affection and our own thought—for God and for others. Then and only then may we as servants of God enter into the feelings of many brothers and sisters.

When our two hands are occupied with some work, we are unable to take up any more. When our heart is already heavily laden, we cannot take in others' burdens. He who is emotionally self-indulgent the least embraces the emotional needs of others the most. Someone may love himself too much; someone may love his family too much. If so, such a person will always be in lack in regard to the matter of loving the brethren. For a man's love is only so great; unless he lays down other loves, he really has no love for the brethren. Yet brotherly love, we know, is one of the cardinal requirements in the work of God.

For this reason, the fundamental condition of divine work is to know the cross. He who does not know the cross is useless in the Lord's work. Without the experiential knowledge of Calvary, one is, without exception, a subjective person. If one does not know the cross, his own thoughts will flow ceaselessly like a river. If one does not know the cross, he can only live in his own feeling. Consequently, it is imperative that we know the cross. There is for us no easy way or shortcut. We must have this basic dealing before God, without which we have no spiritual usefulness. Learn to look for the Lord's merciful dealing with us so that we are delivered from being subjective, from absent-minded woolgathering, and from being insensitive to others' feeling. A workman needs to open himself up to receive people's problems. And by so doing he shall be able to know the words spoken or unspoken, and even their very spirit.

Three

Now as we who would do the Lord's work thus begin to listen, our listening power will be greatly improved. Our understanding will increase to such a degree that the moment a person opens his mouth we know what he is saying. Let us remember that except we are like a piece of white, blank paper within, no additional word can be written on it. To hear and understand what people are saying, we need to be in a state of tranquillity, without our own thought, preconceived idea or personal feeling, so that we may quietly listen. What is essential to a worker is not how much knowledge he has but rather what kind of person he is. Because we have nothing, instrument-wise, but our own self, God will use us as a person to measure other people. But if we are not right, we cannot be used by God. Today we are not using a physical instrument to examine people. It would be much simpler if there were such a physical instrument by which to examine or measure other people spiritually. A thermometer, for example, can easily measure body temperature. But in the Lord's work, that thermometer is we ourselves. You and I as a person must test out other people's state and condition. Consequently, what kind of person we are as God's instrument is of extreme importance. If we are a wrong or bad instrument, nothing can be accomplished, since there is no way for God to use us in dealing with other people. To be a good listener, therefore, is exceedingly essential as a first step towards being an effective workman for the Lord.

For example, someone comes to talk with you to share his difficulty. If you have not been disciplined before God, you would be much inclined to give him some teaching. This is really a very common fault of ours, is it not? Whenever people try to tell us something, do we not often immediately open our mouth to teach them before we feel their spiritual pulse and diagnose their spiritual ailment? Many of us are too impatient to hear them to the end. We make suggestions before we know their problems. We quickly teach and correct after hearing but a few words. How, then, can people possibly receive real help from us?

Yet does this mean that we must sit there and let people talk for three or five hours? That would not be right either. For some people *would* speak for hours and expect you to listen to them at such length. We cannot allow people to talk on indefinitely. Generally speaking, we should give them sufficient time to voice their problem; and hence, we must listen to them for an appropriate time. If we are fairly clear within ourselves, having learned to listen and understand for ten or twenty years, we would hesitate to interrupt people. In order to touch at the root point of a particular situation, a certain amount of time in listening *is* required. Remember that our work is quite complex, inasmuch as we are dealing with living beings who have real problems and serious spiritual perplexities before God. We must never say or interject anything before we have touched the root cause in a given situation. How can we give our judgment when we are not even clear about the situation? In view of the fact that we are dealing with living persons, real problems and spiritual perplexities, we ourselves need to be unprejudiced and quiet before God. The number one reason why many are not able to help others is their inability to listen. Let us therefore ask God to give us grace that while people are speaking to us, we may be able to sit there, listen quietly and understand what is being said. Except we listen carefully, we will never comprehend. Understanding is the key to successful service. It is not easy to speak, but it is even harder to listen. Many preachers are accustomed to speaking, and hence they in particular find it rather difficult to sit down and listen. But this is the first lesson we must all learn.

Failure to be transparent within, to listen, understand and touch the feeling behind the words we hear will cause extreme difficulty for us in our service to the Lord. Let us try to see if we can hear what people say, let us try to see if we can understand them. Outward calm alone is not enough; we need to have that fundamental dealing before God, which is a dealing with our subjectiveness, our thoughts and feelings. Many dealings can be spared, but *this* fundamental dealing is a must. Without it we may be listening outwardly yet be dark within; and therefore, we do not understand. We are to be God's instrument, and if a true instrument, we can know whether a person is hot or cold, normal or abnormal, because we have become that true spiritual thermometer. But if we are not sensitive, we will diagnose wrongly.

There is a mistaken idea abroad among Christians. They often think that as long as a worker can speak, all is well. On the contrary, all is *not* well. In order to do the work of God it is not only a matter of speaking, it is also a matter of the spirit. We need to discern the manifold problems among brothers and sisters and know how to lead them. Can we help them if we are insensitive and dark within, so that we are unable to perceive their actual condition?

When you preach the gospel to a sinner, how do you know whether or not he is saved? Is it through what he says? No, you know in your spirit. How do you know he belongs to the Lord? Is it because he says, "I believe in Jesus, so I am saved"? Do you baptize whoever recites that formula? Not at all; instead, you know inwardly. For you are the spiritual thermometer, that instrument of spiritual discernment. And just as you measure an unbeliever with that thermometer and that instrument, so you measure a child of God with the same instrument. How do you know that the spiritual condition of a child of God is normal? You know and discern by the light in you yourself as the thermometer of God. For this reason, we need to be dealt with by God to the degree that we become a true and effective spiritual thermometer—a true and effective spiritual instrument in God's hands. But if there is a flaw within, we will be prone to err, and the result will be dreadful. What is therefore needed within us is spiritual light.

How sad that many brothers and sisters cannot sit down and listen because they are dark within. Let us realize that we must learn to be quiet and to understand what people say. We must open ourselves to take in other's burdens. And then, by the inner registration we will know wherein lies the problem and how to help.

2 | Must Love All Mankind

One

Those who work the work of the Lord must not only love the brethren but also love *all* mankind. "Whoso mocketh the poor," said Solomon, "reproacheth his Maker" (Prov. 17.5a). All men are created by God; therefore all are to be loved. If a worker does not have sufficient love for the brethren, or if he has the love of the brethren but no love for mankind in general, he is not qualified to serve God. For loving men or showing love to men is an essential quality to have in God's service. All who view people with annoyance and despise them are definitely unfit to be the Lord's servants.

We ought to see that though all men have fallen, they are nonetheless the object of the redemption of our Lord Jesus inasmuch as they were all created by God. In spite of their hardness of heart, the Holy Spirit still convicts them. The Lord Jesus came to this earth; He came to be a man. Like the rest of mankind, He grew up gradually from birth to maturity. For God intends to set up on earth a Model Man, a Representative Man—one upon whom rests all the purposes of God. After the ascension of the Lord Jesus, the church came into being, and yet the church is but the formation of a new man. The whole plan of redemption is to exalt and glorify men.

One day when we come to a deeper understanding of the word of God, we shall find the term "man" more palatable than even the term "the children of God." For we shall realize that God's preordained plan and election is to obtain a glorious man. As we gradually perceive the place of man in God's plan as constituting the focus of His counsel, and when we truly see God humbling himself to be a man, we shall be impressed with the preciousness of man. While our Lord Jesus was on earth He declared that "the Son of man also came not to be ministered unto, but to minister, and to give his life a ransom for many" (Mark 10.45). The word the Lord says here is so plain: the Son of man comes to serve men. The Son of God becomes the Son of man on earth in order to serve men. Thus are we shown the attitude of the Lord Jesus towards mankind.

Many who work for God have a serious deficiency, which is, that they are totally lacking in the love of humanity. They lack the proper respect towards men, and they lack as well a knowledge of the value of man in God's sight. Today we feel elated because we seem to have learned a little love for the *brethren.* Formerly, we loved no one; now, we can show our love towards the brethren by doing something for them. No wonder we are high-spirited. Yet this is far from sufficient. We need to be so enlarged by God that we come to see that *all* people are to be loved and valued. Whether or not you are successful in your future work for God depends chiefly on your attitude towards the value of man. The depth of your work is to be measured by your interest and feeling towards men. By this we do not mean your interest in one or two clever or special persons. We simply mean your interest in "man" *per se*. This is a very significant issue.

The primary sense of Jesus' phrase "the Son of man came" lies in the Lord's tremendous interest in man — so much so as to become a man himself. Such is *His* interest in man; but how about *you*? Many people do not meet your eyes; many people do not arouse your sympathetic feeling. Let us inquire, however, what the Lord's attitude towards them is. He asserts that "the Son of man came." Which means that He takes the place of a son of man among men. He is interested in man, He feels for man, and He values man. His interest in people is so great that He verily stands on the human level in serving mankind. How strange that many brothers and sisters have no interest in man. Should this not arouse our righteous anger? Let us ask ourselves if we really understand what this word "the Son of man came" truly signifies. As we are in the presence of God we ought to see that this word of our Lord Jesus reveals His enormous interest in man. How can we ever think or say that we have no interest in the people we are with? Such an attitude is really preposterous.

Hence in the life of a workman of God there is another basic element in his character formation, which is, that he has an interest in all people. This, however, is not to suggest that he can choose whom among men he will be interested in—that he will only consider a particular person or persons whom he deems as interesting and lovable. No, he must be interested in man *per se*. For let us observe the characteristic of the Lord Jesus, that He had a keen interest in all of mankind. There was such a love in Him towards all of humanity that He could say, "the Son of man came." Suppose we go to a certain place to work for God. If we can say that we come to that place not to be served by the people there but to serve them, then our attitude is proper, our way is correct and our position is right. We shall be like Jesus, the Son of man.

We should always have in mind that as the servants of God we must not withhold our love in a place until some Christian brethren arrive on the scene. All who hold this misconception—namely, that their love is to be reserved for the brethren only—are unable to do the work of God. Let it be known and unequivocally declared that the love of the brethren comes *afterwards*, and that it is a totally different proposition. You need to have a love for the generality of mankind and a compassion towards them. For John 3.16 makes plain that "God so loved the *world.*" What is "the world" here? It refers to all the people in the world, including the unsaved and ignorant. Those whom God loves are the people of the entire world. He loves every one on the earth. If you are not interested in a person whom God loves, and furthermore, if you will love him only after he becomes a Christian brother, your disposition is quite different from the Lord's; and therefore, you cannot serve God. Your heart will need to be expanded to such a degree that you feel that *all* people are to be loved. As long as this one or that one is a person, you love him. And only then shall you be qualified to serve God.

Two

"The Son of man also came not to be ministered unto, but to minister." So continued the Lord Jesus. In other words, the attitude of our Lord here is always that of seeking absolutely nothing from man. We should be interested in all men and love them, but we also should not have any thought of taking advantage of them or of seeking their service. We should not do anything that would embarrass or defraud them, nor should we look to be ministered to.

Perhaps you have reached the stage after many years of education wherein you are able to use the term, "my fellow-men." Yet this term is not meant to be merely a vocal expression; it is meant to signify a sort of feeling. For instance, you have many who are your "fellow-believers." You are aware that they are your brothers and sisters in Christ, and you have a sense of brotherhood towards them. But let us go a step further. Since you live among so many people, do you also ever have a sense of "fellow-men"? How can you serve the Lord if you do not have such an awareness? All who serve God are "big" souls—that is to say, their souls are so big that they embrace all men in their heart. Just here, however, lies a great problem: many of God's workmen lack this basic love for people. If the love of the brethren is so weak among us, how can we talk about the love of men? We will probably select one person out of a hundred—or even out of ten thousand—to love! This proves that we do not have the love of humanity in our hearts.

We ought to remember that all human beings including ourselves are created by God to be fellow-men. Our hearts should therefore be expanded to love all the people whom God has created to be our fellow-men. And this means that we must not defraud them, nor take any advantage of them, nor even look for their service: "for the Son of man also came, not to be ministered unto, but to minister." As Christians who live on earth, we should account it shameful to defraud a fellow-man. It is not only wrong to defraud a *brother*, it is also wrong to defraud *man*—period! Look at the attitude of our Lord Jesus towards mankind. Negatively, He seeks not to be ministered to; He does not entertain even the slightest idea of getting something from man. We, too, must have the same mind continually, that we will not do anything to selfishly gain people's service or support at their expense.

By the command of the Lord, God's children should not take advantage of other people. For the sake of being fellow-men, we must not seek any gain from them. We ought to see before the Lord that all men everywhere are to be loved. And hence, if perchance you have no interest in humanity, then whatever you do before God is going to be very, very limited. For He expects His servants to be of enlarged capacity, to be those who are interested in all mankind. And they shall thus receive grace to serve God.

Three

"The Son of man also came not to be ministered unto, but to minister, and to give his life a ransom for many" (Mark 10.45). "The Son of man came to seek and to save that which was lost" (Luke 19.10). "I came that they may have life, and may have it abundantly" (John 10.10b). Jesus came for all men. He came to minister and to give His life as a ransom for many. This indicates that the purpose of His coming is to serve the world. Of that service, the world of men have a special need which requires His giving His life as a ransom. And accordingly, the Lord Jesus gave His life. In His being a ransom for many, He fulfills the highest and ultimate task of service.

To quote Him accurately, we must see that the Lord Jesus did not say "The Son of man came to give his life a ransom for many"; He instead said, "The son of man came . . . to minister." His aim is serving humanity. For He has an interest in all people; He sees them as those He would love and also serve. He serves to meet the fundamental need of man—the need of a Savior; so He gives His life to be a ransom for many. We are not qualified to do the Lord's work if we merely preach the gospel of His redemption and yet lack the heart to serve the world.

Man is to be loved, hence the Lord comes to serve as the Son of *man*, not as the Son of *God*. He first serves, first loves, *then* gives His life for many. First love, then sacrifice. When you go among people, you cannot preach the sacrifice of the Lord if you do not have love. Do not think that before you can love a person you are to preach to him until that person becomes a brother. Not so. Unless you can appreciate the fact that all human beings are created by God, you really are not in the right spirit to preach sacrificial love to them. We must first *love* men before we can *lead* them to accept the Lord. We should never wait until they have accepted Christ and become brothers and sisters before we begin to love them.

It is a matter of deep regret that many today possess this defect and have this problem. They usually keep back their love until people become their brothers and sisters in Christ. Our Lord, however, was not that way on earth. He first loved men by serving them, and then He laid down His life for them. All who preach the good news of redemption must likewise first love men and then proclaim the gospel to them. Our Lord indeed served and dispensed grace to men first before He ever died for them. May we, too, be interested in all people and sense their preciousness; may we, too, show grace to them before we ever present the redemptive work of the Lord to them.

If our heart is opened by God to see that we are fellow-men, our attitude towards all mankind will be completely changed. We shall feel the preciousness and lovableness of all people. Let me clearly state that it is absolutely essential for you to see the dearness of man in the eyes of God because man is created by Him according to His image. In God's heart all human beings today remain as those who are originally created in His image. And consequently, you must be a person who loves all people before you can go into their midst and serve them with the gospel. Let us see the lovableness and value of human beings before God.

Many brothers and sisters who are engaged in the Lord's work have a wrong attitude towards humanity. They consider the people whom they contact to be a nuisance, a drudgery, a burden or an entanglement. This is a terrible mistake. Let us learn to see before the Lord that man is created by God. Though he indeed be fallen, he nonetheless retains traces of the image of God, and he still has the hope of a glorious future through the gospel of Jesus Christ. In seeing this, we shall then sense that man is to be loved. We shall no longer treat people as an entanglement, a drudgery or a nuisance. Since our Lord has gone to the cross for them, can we love them any the less? One who is really touched by the Lord and who truly understands why He came to this world can readily perceive that human beings are to be loved. It will be impossible for such a person not to love mankind.

Man is to be loved. All his sins can be forgiven; all his weaknesses may be forborne; and all his carnalities can be foreseen. Because we too are sinners, we can therefore understand the tragic story of man. On the other hand, we also know the value of man. Let us not imagine that the Lord Jesus came to die because of the great number of people in the world. For He himself has explained that the shepherd goes out to seek the *one* lost sheep (see Luke 15.3–7). He did not come to seek because ninety-nine sheep had gone astray. To the *good* shepherd, *one* lost sheep is sufficient reason for him to come and to seek. In other words, even if but one person out of the whole world's people is perishing, He is ready to come down from heaven to earth.

Now as a fact of history, He has indeed saved a countless multitude; but so far as the love in His heart is concerned, He seems to come just for that one person, that one lost sheep. The Holy Spirit is as the woman who, told of in Luke 15, sweeps the house and searches diligently for the one lost piece of silver until it be found. He does not wait until, like the woman, all ten pieces are lost before He begins to search for that one lost soul. In the parable of the prodigal, also in Luke 15, the father (representing the Father God) welcomes the one prodigal son who returns. Yet he does not wait until all his sons become prodigals and only then will he welcome them back. No, he welcomes the coming home of even *one* prodigal son. And so with the heavenly Father too. Hence the Lord Jesus shows us in His spoken parables of Luke 15 that He will do the work of redemption to meet the need, if necessary, of but one single person. He will not wait until the many have needs. All this would indicate how interested is our Lord towards the human race.

Therefore, in order to serve the Lord well, you must learn to be interested in people. Without such an interest, you can do little. For even if you do serve, what is done will be very limited inasmuch as your heart is too small in capacity to embrace so many people. Not until your interest in humanity grows and your heart is increasingly enlarged can you understand the meaning of redemption and appreciate the value of man in God's economy. Without this enlargement it is totally unthinkable that such narrow-minded persons as we are can contemplate so great a work. How can we save souls if we do not love them?!? It is impossible to save souls without loving them first. Only when this basic problem is solved can many other problems concerning human beings be resolved. No human lack of knowledge should hinder your love; no hardness of heart should block your love. With love in your heart that has been enlarged, you will not despise anyone; and as a consequence, you shall be brought by God to stand together with your fellow-men.

When some brothers and sisters from urban areas go to the rural villages to serve, they unconsciously take with them a superiority complex towards the farmers. Such an attitude is despicable. Our Lord has not said, "the Son of *God* came"; He said, "the Son of *man* came" (see again Mark 10.45). In order to preach the gospel, one must become a son of man.

Unfortunately, it often happens that when a worker goes to a certain place, he has the feeling of condescending himself. Humbling oneself is a must, but to harbor in one's heart the notion that his very coming among men is itself a humble act is thinking that is totally unacceptable. If you should have a feeling of condescension when among people of less intelligence or of a lower economic or social standing, your humility will not be natural but artificial. From the human viewpoint, while our Lord was on earth He was seen to be a son of Mary; His brothers were James, Joses, Judas, and Simon; and they and his sisters lived among the people. He was known only as the son of man. You, too, must be known simply as a human being. When you go into the midst of people, do not display among them an air of superiority. If so, your attitude is totally wrong. A Christian should never do this. You ought to be as one of them, without ever creating the feeling in them of your condescension. Otherwise, you will not be able to serve them.

We may serve only as "man" to "men." We must never give people a reason to sense that we are trying to condescend ourselves as if we are an altogether different and higher kind of creature. If we do create such a sense in them about ourselves, we are disqualified to be servants of God. In order to serve the Lord, we must truly humble ourselves to the lowest place. In talking with people who are less intelligent or lower on the economic or social scale, we will not be their fellowmen if we position ourselves on a different level than they and give people a different impression.

Unless we humble ourselves to the lowest point, we cannot serve God. We must be so humble that we never harbor any superiority consciousness. No brother or sister may despise a person disadvantaged in terms of education, economic level or social class. In God's creation, redemption and plan, this latter person has the same destiny as anyone else. Only in one thing may we be different, and that is, that, unlike the unbeliever, we know the Lord. Oh, do let us see that many of our attitudes may be wrong. Our whole being, whether in our attitudes, feelings or thoughts, needs to be transformed. We must come to realize that *all* people are equal before God. For if our Lord could come humbly to this earth for them all, can we not also humble ourselves for them? Never make any distinction because of intelligence or any other human factor.

Some may ask, we indeed must not look down upon a less fortunate individual; but suppose we encounter a person who is deceitful, sinful or corrupted—what should be our attitude towards him? The answer is quite simple: you should recall your own days before your salvation. Were you better than that person? If the grace of the Lord should be removed from you, would you be any stronger or purer than he? Who makes you holier? If you were to look at yourself apart from grace, you would not find any difference between yourself and that particular soul. Apart from what grace has done to make you different, you are no different from him at all. You can only bow your head and say, "I am a sinner even as he." Grace must cause you to lie in the dust and pray, "Lord, it is You who have saved me!" Grace will never persuade you to lift up yourself. Quite the contrary, grace will enable you to see that you are the same as those deceitful, sinful and corrupted people. What *really* makes you different is the grace of God, not you yourself. What ever can you boast of, since all you have has been received from God? And if your distinction comes indeed from grace, then you cannot in any way exalt yourself in such grace. Let us praise and offer thanks for the grace of God more; let us not elevate ourselves. In the presence of the Lord, we need to realize that we are just the same as they are; and therefore, we must love them. Though their sins be hateful, nevertheless their person deserves love. And thus shall we cultivate having a large enough heart to lead them to the Lord.

Four

Let us be reminded once again that all who would be used by God must possess certain qualities which are usable to Him. All who may be used of the Lord are interested in people, deeply interested in them. If a worker were to have a larger and warmer heart and to show greater interest in people, his ministry would be greatly increased. How can we go forth to preach the gospel if we are so cold towards humanity and have no interest in them at all? We may indeed go forth to deal with them to save and to win them. Yet what can we do if we have no interest in them? Why do we even go if we consider them to be a nuisance and offensive? If no physician is afraid of seeing patients and if no teacher is fearful of meeting students, then is it not odd if we who preach the gospel are fearful of man!?! Hence all who wish to do the work of the Lord must be interested in all people.

Let us see that you and I are not forced to go forth; we ourselves are to be motivated to contact people by our interest in them. We are to go not because we are persuaded to communicate with people, but because we sense the lovableness and preciousness of man in our heart. We need to realize that all these vast multitudes of people around us are created by God. They are loved and desired by Him. He gave His only begotten Son to them with the hope that they might believe in Him and thus receive life. We differ from them on one point only, and that is, we have believed. Yet we should lead them also to believe. And this we must do by exhibiting the greatest interest in and love for them.

And then shall we have this unending task of serving them. By the mercy of God, we will become useful workmen in His hand.

If anyone wishes to serve God well, this path of which we have been speaking must be straight. Let us never forget that every person has a spirit. In this respect, all are equal before God. We therefore ought to love every soul we meet, and we must therefore desire to serve each and every one. Then, when we walk along the street and meet a person, we will sense and view things quite differently.

Now as a person is enlightened by God to see that his Christian brother and he are born again of the same Father, he will unquestionably exhibit a special feeling towards that brother. By the same token, we workers need to be enlightened to see that both the people at large and we ourselves have been created by the same God. Under such enlightenment, we will manifest an uncommon interest towards any person we meet. Even as already we have a special feeling towards our brothers and sisters because we are conscious that these are our brethren in Christ, just so, we need also to receive another enlightenment from above that informs us that all these countless people around us are our fellow-men. Each one of them is precious, is to be loved, and is worthy of our unending service.

Now with such enlightenment as this, we shall touch the heart of God, inasmuch as His attention is always towards man. Since all of mankind are created by God, it is our privilege to save some of them and to add them to the Church of God. Although the completing and perfecting of the Church is God's ultimate aim, His work today is to gain people. No one who works for the Lord can afford to despise a single soul. Any contempt for a soul, expressed in attitude or in deed, disqualifies a person from being a servant of God. In order to serve Him well, a person not only must not disdain any soul but he also must learn to be a servant of all souls. Let us learn to help all people in various ways; and let us learn to serve willingly and not grudgingly.

Some have the habit of looking down upon those who are supposedly inferior and looking up to those who are supposedly superior. It will be a most shameful thing if such a habit is found among God's servants. We must not exhibit any attitude of contempt towards those whom we consider "inferior." We need to go to God to obtain a revelation of the place and position of all mankind in His sight. We cannot serve the Lord if we fail to have this deficiency solved. We must see the value of man, and so seeing, it will be a great and joyous sight. By perceiving how the Lord came to die for all humanity, we will be characterized by His dying love. We will be able to enter into our Lord's feeling and will sense the loveliness of all men. Only thus shall we show great interest in all of humanity. Otherwise, we are unfit to work for the God who made us all in His very image.

3 | Have a Mind to Suffer

Forasmuch then as Christ suffered in the flesh, arm
ye yourselves also with the same mind . . . (1 Peter 4.1)

One

All who serve God need to possess an additional
characteristic—that of having a mind to suffer (see 1
Peter 4.1). This too is most essential. But before we address this specific question, let us first deal generally
with the attitude of a Christian toward suffering.

The teaching of Scripture is quite plain: God has
no desire to see His people suffer. There is a certain
philosophical concept abroad which posits the notion
that the human body is intrinsically evil—and that
therefore we humans must suffer and not enjoy blessing. People with such a concept view any kind of en-
joyment as something wrong.

As servants of the Lord, however, we go forth to
represent Him. We ought to be clear that the above con-

cept is not a Christian one. The Bible definitely shows us that God has never purposed to have His children suffer. On the contrary, it plainly tells us that the Lord has not withheld any good thing from us: "Jehovah is my shepherd; I shall not want" (Ps. 23.1; see also, 1 Tim. 6.17). The words "I shall not want" here, do not mean that I shall have no need. They simply mean that with Jehovah as my Shepherd, I shall not be in need of any kind. For example, if you have just had a solid meal, and someone offers you a bowl of *congee* (watery rice), you will doubtless say, "I am full, I do not need it." In a similar vein, what the psalmist is saying here is that, having the Lord as my Shepherd, I shall be in lack of nothing. In other words, God does not desire that we be in lack; on the contrary, He wants us to be full; and so, "no good thing does he withhold from those who walk uprightly" (Ps. 84.11).

Beginning at the very outset of the Old Testament record, the Bible consistently reveals to us how God takes care of His people, minimizes their problems and mitigates their sufferings so as to separate them from the heathen nations. Take as just one example the circumstances among the Hebrews in the land of Egypt. The land of Goshen where they lived was different from the rest of Egypt. God's blessing was always present in Goshen. Hence we believers must not bring this kind of suffering philosophy into our Christian faith. Let us not confuse Christianity by mixing non-Christian notions into it. This is something we need to watch.

On the other hand, this is not to suggest that God will not test His children nor discipline them: he does indeed test them and chasten them. Yet we need to distinguish this from the philosophical concept of suffering just mentioned. In ordinary times God usually dispenses grace, taking care of, supporting and supplying His own children with whatever they need. But in times of necessity He will also test and chasten His own. Yet even here, this is not to say that He will try them every day. He only chastens when chastening is necessary. He never chastens on a daily basis or at every moment: He only does so sometimes, not all the time. Our God is habitually mindful of us to provide for our every need. Nevertheless, if we persist in our obstinacy in a given area of life, He will have to allow the trial and discipline to continue — although according to His usual way He loves to deal kindly with us and is unwilling to make us suffer. It is the will of our Father God to give all good things to His children. We may therefore receive and enjoy all which the Lord has given to us.

What, then, is the meaning of the suffering for the saint which we find in the Bible? In the Scriptures we find that to suffer is a path which we deliberately choose to take before the Lord. This is to say that the Lord has indeed provided us with days of abundant grace; but today, for the sake of being God's servants and serving Him, we instead choose this way of suffering. In short, this path is a selected way. It is not unlike what the three mighty men of David did who could have easily followed their leader and lived on peacefully, but once learning of David's longing to taste water from the well by the gate of his home village of Bethlehem, they jeopardized their lives by breaking through the host of the Philistine army to draw water out of that very well (see 2 Sam. 23.14-17). Hence to suffer is something chosen by us; it is not ordained. We *choose* before God to suffer. We are willing to do so for the sake of serving the Lord. According to God's providence, we may not have to suffer many pains; yet because we desire to serve Him, we gladly choose a path which differs from the common one. And this is what is meant by having a mind to suffer. To arm ourselves with such a mind is a basic characteristic of any person who would wish to serve God. Without this willingness, we will not be able to serve well in anything. Lacking this, our service will be very superficial.

Two

Yet, let it be clearly known here that being willing to suffer is not the same thing as suffering itself. It simply means that before God I have a desire of being willing to endure hardship, difficulty or trial for the Lord. I am prepared to do so and will gladly do so for Him. And this is having the mind to suffer. Whoever has this mind may not in fact suffer, yet in his mind and heart he has committed himself to do so gladly for the Lord.

Suppose, for example, that today, God supplies you with food and clothing and better lodging with better furniture. It is not wrong for you to enjoy these things. You may accept from the Lord whatever He has provided; nonetheless, you still possess a heart willing to suffer for Him. Though you do not experience any physical hardship at the moment, nevertheless your mind is still willing to experience that for the Lord. Hence the issue lies not in outward happenings but in your heart desire. When you are in a most favorable situation, do you still possess the mind to suffer? The Lord may not arrange to have us endure hardship every day, but all who work the work of God must not lack the mind to endure such a thing each day. Suffering may not be a daily experience, yet having a mind to suffer must be present daily.

The problem we face is that many brothers and sisters, as well as members of their families, shrink back at the slightest provocation. They do not possess the mind to suffer. When the Lord arranges to let us have a favorable environment, without any lack in material things, and with a relatively healthy body, we can serve Him daily and well. But once we encounter a little trial and meet up with the slightest trivial problem, our whole being collapses. This betrays the fact that we do not have the heart to suffer. How can we possibly stand any test if we do not have such a heart?

Having the *mind* to suffer speaks of my *readiness* before God to suffer. I am willing to go through trial, and I choose the path of hardship. It is *up to the Lord* whether or not to *put* suffering in my path, but on *my part* I am *always prepared* to suffer. Thus when His providential change comes and trial falls upon me, I will not be surprised but rather feel that this is what I should go through in the first place. In the event I can only accept God's *favorable* arrangement and am unable to endure any trial, then as soon as the circumstances shift in the latter direction, I am broken and my work for the Lord ceases. Now this is a clear indication that I do not have the mind to suffer.

Do please understand that work cannot wait for

you. Whether you have food or not, you nonetheless must work. Whether you are clothed or not, you must nevertheless continue serving the Lord. When you are well you work; when you feel uncomfortable you *still* work. You serve whether in health or in sickness. By this shall you find out if you are armed with the mind to suffer or not. Yet this is an awesome weapon, before which Satan is unquestionably bound. Otherwise, once trial and trouble come, your work instantly ceases.

Some brothers and sisters have suffered, and yet they do not see the preciousness of suffering before God. And as a consequence they are not in the least thankful to the Lord. On the contrary, they may at times even murmur and complain. They become apprehensive if such a day does not speedily pass. They may have prayers, but they never give praise. Whatever has come upon them under the discipline of the Holy Spirit they will not gladly accept. They expect such a time to quickly fade away. This kind of attitude plainly manifests their lack of having a heart to suffer.

Allow me to say that if you do not possess the mind to suffer during peaceful days which the Lord has given you, you will only be able to proceed when the way is smooth, because as soon as the road turns muddy, you will stop serving. This ought not to be so. Let me reiterate what was said earlier, that having the mind to suffer is not suffering itself. You may in truth possess such a mind and yet the Lord may not see fit to give you suffering. Even so, if and when you are in fact touched with hardship or trial, you will not shrink back, because within you dwells a heart to suffer.

We need to note, however, that not all who suffer

have the mind to do so. Many are going through difficulty and trial, and yet they may not possess the mind to suffer. So that among those who suffer, there are those with the mind to do so and others without the mind so to do. Quite a number of brothers and sisters cry almost daily for deliverance from the things they must endure. They are daily in distress, hoping day and night that such a time will soon pass away. Such people have no mind to suffer in the midst of hardship.

Therefore, let all who are under trials — whether physical, financial or otherwise — remember this: that what counts before the Lord is not whether you *suffer*, but whether you have the *mind* to suffer. Make no mistake in thinking that because you suffer greatly, you are therefore enduring hardship and trouble for the Lord. Without a doubt your circumstance *is* painful, but it needs to be asked how much of a mind to suffer for the Lord do you really have? Do you choose this path of suffering before the Lord? or are you complaining, annoyed, self-pitying and self-seeking when you do suffer? Let it be plainly understood that people can undergo much heart pain or actual physical trial and yet simultaneously have no mind to do so. Possessing a mind to suffer is a much deeper issue than undergoing the suffering itself. To have the mind to suffer may not issue forth in one suffering outwardly; but by the same token, for a person to suffer outwardly may not mean he has the mind to suffer.

We can also put it this way, that the materially poor may not be spiritually poor, for many who go through much material hardship and trial are rich in the spirit in that they do have a mind to suffer; yet there are many brothers and sisters who, though they might equally be going through difficulty and material hardship, do *not* have a mind to suffer. And should the Lord allow these latter to choose, they would rather not suffer, neither for a month, nor for a day—nay, not even for a moment. They do not possess a heart to suffer.

A person who lacks this character attitude shall find his labor in the Lord limited. For when the outside demand exceeds his ability, he will immediately withdraw. He is unable to sacrifice all. What he treasures he keeps for himself. He can only be engaged in the smoothest service during the most convenient days. He needs the Lord to remove all the obstacles for him so that he may work peacefully. Yet how surprising it is that a person who serves the Lord should make such a demand.

So let us clearly understand what is meant by having the mind to suffer. A brother who is living peacefully may have more of such a mind than he who is actually suffering. In human eyes, of these two brethren, the one under trial is undoubtedly the one who is suffering. Yet in God's eyes, the brother in peace who definitely has the mind to suffer would be more precious to the Lord. This is because what the Lord values the most in His children is not the suffering itself but their having a heart to suffer. Yet because the Lord has no intention of making us suffer, let us not therefore think that our suffering itself has any merit.

May we ever keep in mind that the one thing God requires of us to respond well to is to be willing to have the mind to suffer. We must be armed with this very weapon. Without this as a weapon, we cannot fight the battle for the Lord. We will instead retreat at the least hint of hardship. We will not be able to endure the least pain or pay the smallest price. We will immediately shrink back. In view of this, the question to be put to you is not how much you suffer but how much you are willing to suffer. Naturally we would expect a brother who encounters much pain to have received more grace from God. Even so, we may not be able to find help from that brother simply because we later discover that within him there is no heart to suffer. How totally unwilling he is in this area. He has in truth gone through much trial and tribulation, but he has not learned any lesson before God because his heart is full of rebellion. We are therefore shown the difference here between the mind to suffer and suffering itself. We cannot in any way substitute the latter for the former.

Three

Here we see the dilemma in the Lord's service. Sometimes, for example, in the work which God has called us to do, we find ourselves in physical need because He seemingly has not provided sufficiently for us. What shall we do amidst such trial? Well, if we stop working because of material straitness, might not our Lord be surprised and might He not be justified in asking us what is the basis and reason for our service? So that in God's service, having the mind to suffer is a decisive factor. For you cannot come to the Lord and say you quit because you encounter some unexpected difficulty or trial. No one who serves the Lord may stay home during rain and go forth only after the sun comes out. If you have the mind to suffer, then you will work on in spite of privation, difficulty, pain, sickness, or even approaching death. Possessing a mind to suffer, you will stand up and declare to the devil, "I will work on, no matter what may come!" But if you are inwardly afraid, you will fall away at whatever provocation Satan may cast along your path. If you say, "I am not afraid of hunger," then when Satan threatens you with hunger, you stand firm and the devil flees. If you say, "I am not afraid of coldness," you will stand and Satan must withdraw when the latter tempts you with coldness. But if you should say, "I am afraid of being sick," Satan will make you sick and thus you will be vanquished. Without a mind to suffer, you are subject to Satanic attack at this very point of your fear, and you will be finished. But if you declare, "I am not afraid of sickness," Satan will be bound.

In the light of all this, every one of God's workmen must be prepared before the Lord to go forth with a fearless heart. Whatever may happen—whether it be family trouble, physical ailment, hunger or cold—you shall continue to serve. With the result that the Enemy can do nothing to you. Such an attitude reveals having the mind to suffer. On the other hand, when such an attitude is lacking, you will be tempted with the very thing of which you are afraid. And the consequence will be that you will invariably withdraw from the work of God. In short, you become unusable.

May we all say to God, "For the sake of Your love and because of the grace You have given me today, I am fully committed to Your work. Come heaven or come hell, I will work on. Whether competent or incompetent, I shall pursue the work to its very end."

Without such a heart as this we will be open to the attack of the Enemy at our point of weakness. We will quickly be finished and reduced to ineffectiveness. For this reason we must plead with God to show mercy towards us and grant us this mind to suffer. To have *this* mind is to be inwardly ready for the Lord regardless what event or future circumstance may overtake us. Having such a mind to suffer does not necessarily automatically incur suffering; probably, there will be no suffering; yet an inward determination anchors us firmly. And whoever has this inner assurance is fortified against trouble of any kind. But whoever lacks such certitude will collapse when confronted with trouble.

Have you now realized the absolute necessity for having such a mind? The way of service lies not in suffering, but in possessing the mind to suffer. That is to say, you thank God for hunger and nakedness as well as for food and clothing. These things create no difficulty in your life. Neither good nor bad represents any problem to you at all. Please understand that Christians do not ever *seek* to suffer, they must simply have a mind to suffer. They are prepared to press on in the face of whatever difficulties come their way. But if this should remain an unsettled issue in your life, then nothing is settled.

Let us take what may occur in travel as an example of what we have been saying here. It is true that some people may be physically weak and need to sleep on a better bed. But if you as God's servant insist that you must sleep on a more comfortable bed because of your feebleness, then Satan can attack you at this very point and cause you to have an uncomfortable bed to sleep on. To have the mind to suffer denotes that, regardless the condition of the bed, you will work on. If the Lord so arranges for you to sleep on a better bed, do not prefer to sleep on the floor. You should sleep on any kind of bed He provides for you. No matter what the condition of the bed is, you continue to serve and will not shrink back. Such an attitude is what the Scriptures call having the mind to suffer.

Some brother may be living under a poorer material condition. By this alone it cannot be assumed that he has the mind to suffer. Do not conclude that the materially poorer brother must certainly be one who possesses a greater mind to suffer than a materially better-off brother. Only those who have truly consecrated themselves to the Lord are in possession of such a mind. Such a heart to endure suffering knows no measure nor end. You may go to one place and sleep on the floor. You may go to another place, and there is no floor for you to sleep on but only a pile of hay in the mud. What will you do in such a circumstance? Someone may accept it with great reluctance. Nevertheless, though he suffers, his suffering has a measure or boundary to it. He may be willing to sleep on the floor, but that is the extent to which he can manage the situation — he cannot lower himself further by sleeping in the hay on the muddy ground. By this he seems to say that his standard of living is already low enough and cannot go any lower. This only affirms that he has the *fact* of suffering in his life but not the *mind* to suffer.

On the other hand, there are other brothers and sisters who in their daily living enjoy more material comforts and yet when their standard of living is compelled by circumstance to be lowered, they can take it in stride as though nothing has happened. They can sleep on the floor or even on muddy ground spread with hay. They utter not a word of reluctance or complaint, for they gladly accept the provision. Now *this* is having a mind to suffer. And God will choose such people to serve Him.

So our issue today is not over how much we suffer but over what is the measure or boundary to our endurance. Suffering may not be necessary for us, but having the mind to suffer is a *must*. The Lord will not purposely put us in continuous trial or hardship; He only desires to create in us a mind to suffer. No one who goes forth to serve God can be strong without possessing this kind of mind. Else he will be a feeble workman. He will pity, favor and shed tears for himself at the least difficulty or inconvenience. He will sigh and say, "How have I fallen into such a trying situation!" This reminds me of the instance when on one occasion a sister was weeping. Another sister who had served the Lord many years asked her: "But for *whom* are you weeping?" Alas, many weep for themselves. They bemoan the fact that, being so lovely and so precious, they have now been demoted into this uninviting, unpleasant place or situation. So they weep for themselves. Such people are the weakest, and they are the quickest to fold when the going gets rough.

The question before you is this: when trial and pain come your way, where is your heart? On the one hand is your hardship; on the other hand is the Lord's work. In the event you do not have the mind to suffer, you will immediately sacrifice the work of the Lord. You will muse, "How can I possibly take care of the Lord's work when I can hardly take care of my distress!" Oh, at all costs, we must arm ouselves with the mind to suffer, for there is no question that our suffering shall indeed subside if we lay down the work; but in so doing God's work will suffer loss.

Here, then, is the problem: when there is a lack of a mind to suffer, or when there is no mind present to suffer at all, Satan is able to tempt us to desert our work for the Lord at any time. Yet we are to be people who maintain the glory of God. Come life or come death, we must fulfill our duty. We have to finish our course and persevere to the end. This that I have said is not meant to imply that it is expected that our laboring brothers and sisters are to suffer. Under ordinary situations, our need for food, clothing and lodging is legitimate and good in God's sight to be met. We do not in the slightest encourage brothers and sisters to seek out sufferings to bear, nor would we ever put suffering upon anyone: we would that God would supply our every need so that we would lack in nothing. Yet we still maintain that to have a mind to suffer is an absolute necessity for those who are God's workmen. On the one hand, we are aware that God would not withhold any good thing from us; on the other hand, we must possess the mind to suffer. If not, we shall fall at the least inconvenience or trouble.

Four

How much of a mind to suffer must we possess? The demand of the Scripture is: "faithful unto death"

(Rev. 2.10c). In other words, we must be able to endure anything, even death itself. We are not advocating extremes here. Yet having the mind to suffer is never moderately defined in God's word. If moderation is called for in the case of some of you workers because of excess, then let the Lord, the Church or the more matured brethren temper your excess. But so far as you are concerned, you must give your *all*. How can you ever serve if *you* temper yourself? There is no way for you to work. A person who looks upon his own life as precious and loving and who always holds his life in his own hand is very limited in the work of God. Every one of us who would be in God's service must be prepared to be faithful unto death. This is the only path we can travel. It goes without saying that the Lord will not ask you to die because of your faithfulness. Nonetheless, the preserving of our life is up to the Lord and is not a matter for our concern. Should the Lord so order, that is His business. On our side, we must always be ready to lay down our life. No matter how painful, we must learn to endure.

Let me say this, that if you live your own life, you will not be able to be faithful unto death. Yet this is the basic demand of the Lord. The mind to suffer should be so strong in us that we may say, "O Lord, it is fine with me if death should come! I am willing to lay down my life for You, totally unmindful of any distressful situation." God needs such "violent" ones to serve Him (see Matt. 11.12) — those who would dare to put their lives on the line. Let us not worry about how we can avoid being extreme. That is another matter. Here we must realize that though it is impossible for us to pre-arrange everything, it is absolutely necessary that we have this mind to suffer before God. We must be prepared to give our all in the face of outside trouble or physical weakness. If we will not be "violent" with ourselves, then we can do nothing. Let us tell the Lord, "O Lord, I am willing to give my all. Hereafter nothing can hinder my serving You. Come death or life, come sorrow or joy, with You I have cast my lot."

This one thing is most effective—that of serving the Lord even unto death. The more you stand on *this* ground, the less the Enemy has any way with you. Alas, how people love their own selves. A little pain draws out rivers of tears and eruptions of sighs. Were we not to love ourselves, these tears and sighs would vanish from the scene. In order to travel this road God's servants must be "violent" people. They must say to the Lord, "Lord, whether You have ordained for me to suffer or not, I am fully prepared to suffer." Again and again I would say that suffering is a limited matter, whereas the mind to suffer is an *un*limited one. The amount of hardship or trial the Lord allows you to endure is measurable, but the extent of your readiness to suffer before the Lord is to be *im*measurable. On the other hand, if your mind to suffer is measurable, then you do not really have the mind to suffer. Any limit here renders such a person ineffective in the Lord's work. Anything less than what God demands makes one's service unacceptable to Him.

Never entertain the thought that the mind to suffer is restricted to only a certain measure of suffering. No, no, it is to be measureless, even unto death. Otherwise, Satan will be able to tempt you and make you fall.

"They overcame him [Satan] because of the blood of the Lamb, and because of the word of their testimony; and they loved not their life even unto death" (Rev. 12.11). What can the Enemy do if your conscience is void of offence, you have the word of the testimony of Christ's victory, and you love not your life even unto death? The Enemy has no way in the slightest to deal with those who love not their lives in that way!

We all know the story of Job. The reason why Satan attacked him so fiercely is because God's Enemy just could not believe that a man would not seek to preserve his own life for the Lord's sake. Hence he challenged Jehovah, saying, "Skin for skin, yea, all that a man hath will he give for his life. But put forth thy hand now, and touch his bone and his flesh, and he will renounce thee to thy face" (Job 2.4-5). Satan knew that if he touched Job's life and the latter loved his life, then God's Enemy would have his way. How very clear are the implications of the words in Revelation 12.11: Satan is at his wit's end towards those who love not their lives even unto death.

The failure of God's workmen can be plainly perceived right here—that they love their lives too much. Let us ask ourselves which is more important, the work of God or our own life? our duty to God or our own life? people's souls or our own life? the Church of God or our own life? the testimony of God on earth or our own life? Those who love themselves cannot serve the Lord: and those who suffer may not necessarily be serving the Lord. Only those who have the mind to suffer, who have an unlimited measure of the mind to suffer, who have a mind that "love[s] not their life even unto death"—these, and these alone, are qualified to serve God.

Today, let us offer ourselves afresh to the Lord, not offering ourselves to suffer, but simply offering ourselves to give our all. The Lord may not have destined us to be martyrs, yet we must have the mind to suffer even unto a martyr's death if that be His will. Let us acknowledge and confess how often the failure of our work can be traced to our indolence, self-protection and lack of self-denial. Do not presume that people are blind, that the eyes of other brothers and sisters are closed. Let us realize that they can easily detect whether we are giving our all or keeping back something.

When the Lord calls us, He calls us to put all on the altar. May He be gracious to us that none of us will so treasure his or her life as to be unwilling to lay it down. From the depths of our hearts we must cultivate the habit of not loving or pitying ourselves. Otherwise, our work will be circumscribed. The measure and extent of our having the mind to suffer will determine the measure and extent of our spiritual work for the Lord. Any limitation in having this mind limits the scope of spiritual service. It also limits the blessing to people. We need not use any other standard by which to measure God's blessing than that of having the mind to suffer. And with a measureless mind to suffer there shall come an unlimited scope of blessing.

4 | Disciplining the Body

I do all things for the gospel's sake, that I may be a joint-partaker thereof. Know ye not that they that run in a race run all, but one receiveth the prize? Even so run; that ye may attain. And every man that striveth in the games exerciseth self-control in all things. Now they do it to receive a corruptible crown; but we an incorruptible. I therefore so run, as not uncertainly; so fight I, as not beating the air: but I buffet my body, and bring it into bondage: lest by any means, after that I have preached to others, I myself should be rejected. (1 Cor. 9.23–27)

One

In this passage of Scripture, verse 23 reads in part: "I do all things for the gospel's sake." Paul indicates the way of those who would preach the gospel and serve God. In addition, verse 27 includes these words: "I buffet my body and bring it into bondage." From this we can discern what is the basic demand required of a servant of God towards his own self. And in verses 24 to 27, Paul shows us how he himself buffets his own body to bring it into subjection.

At the very outset of our discussion we would wish to make clear that the buffeting of one's body spoken of by Paul is not at all meant to signify a kind of asceticism. What Paul asserts here is something entirely different from the concept which some people embrace that posits the unbiblical notion that the body is an encumbrance and that only one's emancipation from it can truly bring good news. In the thought of the ascetic, the body is deemed to be the root of all evils; and consequently, whoever would ill-treat his body would indeed be delivered from sin. Yet the Bible never regards the body as an encumbrance to be gotten rid of; it never teaches that the body is the source of evil. Quite the contrary, the Scriptures tell us in this very same letter that our body is a temple of the Holy Spirit (6.19). Our body is to be redeemed, and one day we shall have a glorious body. So that when—in paraphrasing Paul—we mention this matter of buffeting the body to bring it under control, we must never associate it with the misconception to be found in asceticism. For if we inject such a notion into our Christian faith we change the very character of Christianity. People may indeed commit sin by means of the body; and they can still sin however drastically they deal with their body; nevertheless, the body itself is not the source of sin.

Paul shows us in 1 Corinthians 9 that one who would be a workman of God must solve a problem— that of his body. The opening words, "I do all things for the gospel's sake" (v. 23a), indicate that the ground the apostle takes is that of preaching the gospel. What must he do in order to preach the gospel? Verses 24–26 describe this which he must do. And in verse 27 he points out what he has done — namely, that he has buffeted his body and brought it into subjection. According to the original Greek, "buffet" literally signifies to bruise, to strike under the eye; hence, to beat the face black and blue. So that the meaning here is to subdue one's body, as though beating it severely so as to make it one's slave in obedience to him who would be a minister of the gospel. This does not, however, imply using one's hands literally to pummel or beat his physical body. It is not at all to be construed as "severity to the body" that is mentioned negatively by Paul in Colossians 2.23. Rather, it is an exercise or discipline that is done so that Paul might not, "after [he had] preached to others, ... be [himself] rejected" or disqualified.

To a servant of God, this discipline as described by Paul of buffeting his body and bringing it into subjection is a very fundamental principle of living. Every servant of the Lord should live in this way. For how can anyone serve God if his body is *not* in subjection to him? And thus Paul solves this problem presented by the body by buffeting it and bringing it under control. And hence we see that the sentence of verse 27 ("I buffet my body, and bring it into bondage") serves as the subject; whereas verses 24–26 serve as the explanation. The former (v.27) tells us the what, while the latter (vv.24–26) explains the how.

Two

"They that run in a race run all . . ." (v.24a). Paul uses the competitive sport of running as an example. God's servants who work, as well as other Christians who serve, are as runners in a race. All are running: none is an exception. "But one receiveth the prize. Even so run; that ye may attain" (v.24b). In a physical race, only one person receives the prize, but in the spiritual race which we run, each and every one has the chance of winning the prize. This is where our race differs from the other. Paul uses the illustration of running in order to bring in the word which follows in verse 25.

"And every man that striveth in the games exerciseth self-control in all things" (v.25a). What Paul now stresses is that in order to win in the games, one must disicpline himself and exercise self-control in all things. He may not indulge himself inordinately in eating or sleeping. We know that athletes who are to compete in games must undergo very strict discipline during their training. What they can eat or cannot eat is clearly prescribed. When to sleep and when not to sleep are definitely defined. Before the games they are not allowed to drink wine or to smoke. And there are many other restrictions. At the games they must keep many stringent rules. Hence every man who strives in the races must exercise self-control in all things. Some people may object to these rules and declare that they cannot exist without smoking or drinking or carousing. Nevertheless, it is imperative that everyone in the games have absolute control over his body—everyone must "exercise control in all things."

Disciplining the Body

What are the things which must come under control? There must be control over the various demands of the body so that there be no excessive liberty. For in a race, the body is for one purpose only, and that is, to run the race. It is not for eating or clothing or smoking or drinking or sleeping. It is for running. Many runners have to refrain from eating food containing too much carbohydrates, not because such foods are unhealthy but because these are worthless — nay, even deleterious — for running. A runner must be temperate in all things. He must "buffet [his] body and bring it into bondage" — the discipline starts with the body. Even so, we who are in a spiritual race must likewise realize that our bodies need to be under control. They must be responsive to you and me. All the functions of our bodies are gathered up to perform one feat, which is, to run to win.

"Now they do it to receive a corruptible crown; but we an incorruptible" (v.25b). In order to receive a corruptible crown, people are willing to discipline themselves. Should we, who are to receive an *in*corruptible crown, be any less disciplined? The "corruptible crown" mentioned here refers to the flowery laurels with which the Greeks in classical times had crowned the winners of their races. Such laurels of fresh flowers would obviously fade away in a few short days. Yet these runners wished to undergo a long period of training with the hope of gaining just such fleeting crowns as these.

Let us notice the comparison given by Paul: They run on a race course, whereas we run in the world as the course. They run physically; we run spiritually in serving God. They all run but only one receives the prize; but if we run we all may be rewarded. The prize they receive is a corruptible crown; the prize we receive is an incorruptible one. The contrasts between the two are sharp, and yet in one aspect there is sameness. This is what is implied in verse 25: they who run in either kind of race must "exercise self-control in all things." The control over the body is the same. Just as athletes who run in a race require the control of the body, so we who preach the gospel as servants of the Lord must exercise control over the body too. Though the objectives differ, the control over the body is the necessary element to success in both.

"I therefore so run, as not uncertainly: so fight I, as not beating the air" (v.26). Here Paul informs us that his running is not without a goal. He knows to where he is running. He buffets his body, not beating the air. We need to view verses 26 and 27 together. In verse 26 he says he does not run uncertainly. He does not shift his course from the right to the left or vice versa. No, he runs in a fixed direction. Neither is he boxing the air, for in the next verse he points out that he beats his own body. As we mentioned before, "buffet" in Greek means to beat the face black and blue. It is therefore a strong blow, not a light pat, inasmuch as the latter would not result in the face becoming black and blue. Why does Paul deal so severely with his body? Quite plainly, that his body may be in subjection to him. "Bring it into bondage" means making the body my slave, which also means putting it under subjection — that is, under my control. Hence the *end* is to "bring it into bondage"; the *means* is to "buffet my body." I must discipline the body till it serves me and not I it.

If in fact you have not learned this lesson, it is expedient that you spend a few more years learning this control over the body before you step out into service. All who serve God must have their body respond to them. The Bible shows us that working for the Lord is not a simple matter. Do not fancy that a person who likes to preach from the pulpit is a servant of God. Nothing could be further from the truth. For Paul convinces us that only those who "buffet [the] body and bring it into bondage" may serve God. In the event your body does not listen to your will, you may have to learn this lesson well before God. Do not presume to think that with a little desire to work for the Lord you are qualified to serve. A servant of the Lord must buffet his body to make it responsive. Otherwise, he is not of much usefulness to the Lord.

Three

What, then, is meant by this phrase, to "bring it into bondage" or subjection? First of all, we should know what are the demands of the body. It has its definite requirements. For instance, eating and drinking, resting, sleeping, comfort, clothing, care in time of sickness, and so forth. All these are required by the body. What is therefore meant by subduing the body is that through my daily disciplining of it I am able to make it listen to me in times of work or running. If I am in the habit of indulging myself, then in the time of running I shall discover that none of the members of my body, neither

my feet nor my hands, nor even my lungs, will listen
to me and respond to the demands of the race. It requires a long period of training to make the body
responsive; otherwise, it is futile to expect it to respond
to the call of the moment. If training is lacking and
the body has not been buffeted, how can you rely on
its service when it is needed? When you are ready to
work, you will find you have no control over your body
nor are you able to resolve its demands.

Do not think that as long as your spiritual life is
normal you are able to serve. You must also inquire concerning your body. This is shown to us by Paul. Here
we are not asking if your body is healthy or not. What
we would inquire of here is whether or not it listens
to you. Are you able to subdue it and subject it to your
command? Unless you are, you have no way to serve
God in preaching the gospel. Such training is not accomplished instantaneously. Some spiritual issues may
in truth be resolved instantly, but others such as "buffeting my body" may take years, perhaps even five to
ten years. People who are habitually loose in this area
may require a long period to be able to discipline
themselves strictly.

For example, the body needs sleep. There is nothing
wrong or sinful about this; it is unquestionably a
legitimate requirement of the body. God gives us night
to sleep. Sleep is a necessity. How can anyone work if
he does not sleep? Yet the one who has buffeted his
body into obedience is capable of *not* sleeping temporarily during a time of special need. This is what is
meant by "buffeting my body and bringing it into bondage." I may have arranged to have eight hours of sleep

daily according to the necessary care of my body. But for the sake of tempering my body, as though I beat it until it listens to me, I am able not to sleep today if I so desire.

On that fateful night in Gethsemane, our Lord explicitly asked three of His disciples, "Watch with me." But they went to sleep. So He asked of Peter, "What, could ye not watch with me one hour?" (see Matt. 26.38,40) The Lord wanted them to keep guard with Him, but they fell asleep. They could not watch for even an hour. Is it wrong to sleep? Certainly not, for sleep is reasonable and necessary. Yet whenever the Lord places a demand upon us, then that which is necessary must give way, or else it will hinder or even terminate God's work. Hence anyone who insists that he must have his sleep under *whatever* circumstances is unable to serve God.

This is not to suggest that he who serves the Lord must not sleep every night. For then he would be an angel. But you are not an angel, and you therefore need to have good nights of rest. Nevertheless, due to your following the Lord and learning to subdue your body, you are capable of losing a night or two of sleep in a time of emergency. This is called "buffeting the body and bringing it into bondage."

What is a race? Do people run it daily and hourly? We all know that walking is the ordinary mode for motion, whereas running, or running a race, is extraordinary. Walking is a common demand, for we walk step by step daily. Running, or running a race, though, is not a daily affair. In running, we are required to go faster than in our ordinary walking. The normal function of the body is for walking, but running demands extra strength. In the latter case, therefore, the ordinary bodily function is accelerated for special use. The body needs to respond to the higher demand, since besides its normal function, it must take up additional work. Thus running calls for an exceptional summons from the body, whereas ordinary walking does not require so much energy from it.

Now in a similar manner, we may ordinarily sleep eight hours. In the event, however, that we are called to work four more hours in the day, we will only sleep four hours. And this is what, spiritually speaking, Paul meant when he spoke of running a race. It means extra demand is placed upon us who would seek to serve the Lord. Now the three disciples could not watch for an hour. And our Lord immediately pointed out the underlying cause, which was, that for them "the spirit indeed is willing, but the flesh is weak" (Matt. 26.41b). What can a willing spirit do if the flesh is weak? The spirit may be willing, but the flesh wants sleep. Yet this would be just as useless, of course, were the spirit to be *un*willing with the flesh still wanting sleep. It is not enough simply to have a willing spirit; the body needs to be equally willing. If the latter is unwilling and falls to sleep, this shows that it has not been subdued. The unyieldedness of the body renders the willing spirit ineffective.

Yet this can never be meant to imply that the body is the root of sin or that it is an encumbrance. It merely declares that for the sake of serving God, sometimes we have to place an extra demand upon the body, and from which we fully expect cooperation. This, then, is what is meant by "bringing the body into bondage." We must learn to cause our body not only to meet the ordinary demands of life but to cause it to respond as well to those extraordinary demands required when serving God.

When the Lord Jesus was on earth He was quite able to receive without weariness Nicodemus who came to seek Him at night. Moreover, several times He spent the whole night in prayer. All these circumstances made excessive demands upon Him to keep awake. It goes without saying that we do not condone the practice of God's children engaging in whole night prayer too frequently. However, we consider it a shame if those who have learned to serve God *never* spend a whole night in prayers. On the one hand, we should not *habitually* pray the whole night through, because that would be wrong and hurtful to the body. But on the other hand we do reckon it strange if those who claim to be God's workers never once over a span of ten or twenty years in the Lord's service ever use a whole night to pray. We must not be excessive in promoting frequent whole nights of prayer lest our body suffer and our nerves become strained. We deem it to be abnormal for people not to pray in the daytime but pray instead at night, thus foregoing needful sleep in the process. Yet we also deem it questionable if God's workmen never once pray for a whole night.

Though as we have already said, *running a race* is not a daily affair, *training* is. One needs to be trained to such an extent that his body is no longer rebellious but is responsive. The lack of such control over the body will mean that in time of laboring for the Lord, sleep will be the first important consideration to you and it will thus become your master. You may probably be able to do some work if sleep is not vital, but you can do nothing if your sleep is affected. Hence to subdue the body is a necessary exercise for God's servants. Whenever the Lord commands and the environment demands, I am able to set aside my body's requirements temporarily and summon forth an extra supply of energy and strength from it. Instead of my yielding to the body, the latter is yielded to me and follows my direction. Otherwise, I am a person of self-love and I am therefore useless in the work of God.

Let us take eating as another example. We doubtless remember how often our Lord so labored that He had no time to eat. He never allowed His eating to become a problem for Him. This is not to suggest, though, that He never ate, because we know He did eat properly in ordinary times. Even so, He was capable of foregoing eating when needs of ministry were placed before Him. And this is called the yielding up of the body or bringing it into subjection. We are not to be those who cannot work without eating. Unfortunately there are many people who cannot do so. Without a doubt eating is a necessity for us: we must indeed take care of our body: nevertheless, amidst special circumstances we may bring our body into subjection and not eat.

We recall how the Lord Jesus once sat by Jacob's well in Samaria. It was at noontime, and the disciples had gone to the nearby city to buy food. While at the well He saw a Samaritan woman coming to draw water. Jesus asked her to give Him some water to drink, and

He told her about the living water. Yet we do not see the woman giving water to the Lord to drink, even though it was at noonday and certainly the time to drink and eat. Instead, the disciples, upon their return, found our Lord still talking to this spiritually needy Samaritan woman whose soul was bitter and thirsty. He was explaining in detail to her what this other, living water of His was. Does this not show us that at a time of eating one can still do the work of God well without food? If we go to a place on behalf of the Lord and we are unable to work because we are hungry or because there is a lack of food available, it is evident that our body is unserviceable. Let me reiterate that we do not wish to be seen as going to an extreme here by foregoing eating frequently. Yet we *do* wish to maintain that in exceptional times we are and must be able *not* to eat. Food is not so important that we cannot spare one meal! On the contrary, we are to be master of our body. It should listen to *us*. Our body must not rule *over* us. And this is the subduing of the body.

According to Chapter 3 of Mark's Gospel we are told that at one point the multitude had so surrounded the Lord Jesus that He could not so much as eat bread. And when His friends heard it, they went out to lay hold of Him to rescue Him from the situation, "for they said, He is beside himself" (see vv.20–21). Our Lord, however, continued to work; yet not because He was mad but because the multitude had need. When there was need, He was able to lay aside everything — even eating and drinking. Let us therefore realize that all who are unable to lay themselves aside in time of work can do very little for God. In the hour of urgency, we ought to exhibit three percent of excess—three percent of "madness." If necessary, we are capable of restraining our body, without being controlled by it.

The Bible definitely indicates to us that during times of need God's people should fast. Fasting is that exercise which suspends temporarily the legitimate demand of the body. Sometimes we fast before God that we may devote ourselves completely to pray for a certain matter. We do not endorse the formal fasting of three or five times a week, but neither do we feel that it is commendable for a Christian never to have fasted in eight or ten years. Our Lord has dealt with this matter of fasting in His so-called Sermon on the Mount, and it bears some re-reading. We lack something if we do not fast. The true meaning of fasting is to subdue our body.

Let us take as another example the matter of comfort. This too is a demand of the body. It is not wrong for those who serve God to lead in ordinary times a life that includes relative comfort. Nonetheless, we should not permit the body to dictate to us when some discomfort in God's work arises. How can we serve if our body disobeys us? Some brothers and sisters change their place of dwelling often; yet not because the Lord so orders, but because they are unhappy with their former dwelling—it being found uncomfortable and/or unappealing. And thus, the pursuit of comfort becomes their way of life. It is comfort that guides their path. Such people are useless in the hand of God. Let us learn not to live such a life of comfort. We praise God if our Lord should so arrange that under the discipline and ordering of the Holy Spirit we are given a comparatively comfortable living; but we also continue to serve if the

Lord should otherwise so order our steps that we are not able to live comfortably and our body accordingly follows us.

We are not to be viewed as extremists here. It is permissible for us to live more comfortably in ordinary days, but it is required that we be able to endure discomfort more than others if the Lord so orders. Some brothers and sisters can only live comfortable days. A slight decrease in their living standard finishes them. They are not of much use to the Lord. As we run our spiritual race of serving God, we must have our body in subjection. We can live at any place under any environment. The subduing of my body means that I am not affected by changing environment. I can labor on if the work of God requires me to live at a much lower standard of living. Otherwise, I will draw back the moment the environment fails to be in harmony with my customary way of living. Yet this does not suppose, however, that those brothers who usually exist at a lower standard of living may necessarily pass the test either. Many of these brothers will find it unbearable for their body should they be required by God to live at a lower living standard than even the already lower standard to which they have been accustomed. It is all because people — at whatever usual level of comfort — love their own selves too much and have not learned how to keep the body under.

Let us further apply this principle to the example of clothing. We should indeed eat well and dress warmly yet we must not be too attentive to our outward attire. We know that John the Baptist was not one who dressed fashionably. Hence the Lord, while discussing John, told His disciples: "Behold, they that wear soft raiment are in kings' houses" (Matt. 11.8b). You could never see such fashion in John. Unfortunately, today many brothers and sisters pay too much attention to clothing as though they cannot live without maintaining a certain and better-than-necessary standard. Naturally, we are not advocating that God's servants should dress in rags, for this would not glorify the Lord. We should dress properly and do so in such a way as to meet the body's regular needs. However, in times of urgent necessity, such as Paul described in terms of "both hunger, and thirst, and . . . naked[ness]" (1 Cor. 4.11a), we nonetheless keep on serving God. Clothing will not be a problem and should not affect the Lord's work if a servant of God is so disciplined in his ordinary days that his body is in subjection to him.

Let us consider sickness as still another illustration of this principle of subjecting the body to our rule. In times of illness or weakness, the body seems to demand more care. Yet many who work for the Lord love themselves so much that they stop working if they encounter but the slightest ailment. Had Paul been like these people and had he not resumed working until the trouble with his eyes had been cured, he would probably have never written many of his epistles. He would not have written the epistle to the Galatians for sure, because he wrote it at a time when his eyes troubled him severely. For did he not mention therein: "See with how large letters I write unto you with mine own hand" (6.11)? Again, if Paul should have waited until his eyes had been completely recovered, he would most likely not have labored at making tents, since tentmaking, as we know, greatly requires the close use of the eyes. Yet he preached in the day and made tents at night. He did not stop because of eye trouble. Likewise, if Timothy had waited until his stomach had gotten well, the work which he successively did after Paul left the scene, would most certainly have come to an end, because his stomach problem was a chronic matter with him.

Here let us learn one thing: to take care of our body on the one hand but on the other to not love ourselves at those times of inordinate work requirements on God's behalf. Whenever we are faced with a divine work demand, we must lay aside the demand of the body and respond to the demand of the work. There is no question that sickness requires rest and care; nevertheless, even a sick body must respond to the demand of divine work. To "buffet my body and bring it into bondage" is a condition for service. If we cannot use our body to serve the Lord, with what else can we serve? In case a servant of the Lord is quite ill and the Lord makes no special demand on him, it is well for that servant to nurse his sickness carefully. The Church knows how to treat him, and his fellow-workers also know how to look after him. However, should the work demand and the Lord command, then he should not be bound by his sickness. In that event, we, like him, have no time to be sick, we are even able to lay aside the sickness temporarily. This, too, is something we need to learn before God.

Yet this is not only to be true with sickness; it is to be true with pain as well. Sometimes we suffer the latter, it being so terrible as to be beyond our body's endurance. During ordinary times we will take proper care in accordance with the need of the body. But should the Lord command us to work, then we will work in spite of pains. Our body must listen to us. Sometimes we need to lift up our head and declare to the Lord, "Lord, once again I make my body listen to me, once again I cannot yield to its demand."

The problem of sex is no different. Sexual demands may not necessarily have to be satisfied. We must learn to put the work of the Lord first.

Let us look a little at Paul's condition.

> Even unto this present hour we both hunger, and thirst, and are naked, and are buffeted, and have no certain dwelling-place; and we toil, working with our own hands: being reviled, we bless; being persecuted, we endure; being defamed, we entreat: we are made as the filth of the world, the offscouring of all things, even until now. (1 Cor. 4.11-13)

Please notice the phrase "even unto this present hour" in verse 11. It conveys the thought of continuation. We are shown that Paul's body always listened to him; none of these troubles deterred him. In 1 Corinthians 6.12-20 he mentioned two things in particular: one was food, the other was sex. He pointed out that there is no need to always gratify the body. Whether in the matter of sex or food, Paul told us we are not obligated to follow the requirements of the body. In chapter 7 of the same epistle, he clearly showed us further how men are not obliged to please the body in the area of sex; and in chapter 8, showed us further how people are not bound to favor the body in eating.

Hence what is meant by buffeting the body and bringing it into bondage? It means I subdue my own body, I "bruise" or "beat" my own body so as to bring it under my control. As we go forth to serve God, oftentimes we shall have to bridle its demands. Yet are we able to resist its demand when the work of God requires us to do so? Without any question, all the needs as well as the supplies of life are created by God. The body has its legitimate requirements; even so, none of its demands must hinder us from performing acceptable service to God.

Four

In spite of what has been said, however, I would not want you ever to conceive the notion that you may be unmindful about the body's demands. You must know and understand that recklessness and care are totally different. You should *take care* of your body; nevertheless, you must also *control* it. To subdue the body does not suggest that you are to refuse to eat when hungry; it simply means you at times are able *not* to eat when hungry. You should take good care of your body; but should your eating reach the point where it becomes an unbreakable habit, then you are unable to work when you are not provided with your regular food. We do not condone asceticism and we do not deem the body to be the source of evil. Quite the contrary, we confess that the demands of the body are placed in us by God. We also acknowlege our body to be the temple of the Holy Spirit. Nevertheless, we are not obliged to gratify in each and every instance whatever the body demands. We are not advocates of no dress, no food or no sleep as a normal way of living. If possible, we should be sufficiently clothed, sufficiently fed, and sufficiently provided with sleep. Yet there is a vast difference between the clothing, eating or sleeping of those who have subdued their body and of those who are undisciplined.

Today's problem lies in the fact that many brothers and sisters never bridle their body. The lack of strict control over it results in murmuring or desertion under the pressures of divine work. Accordingly, we need to learn to endure, and to say to the Lord, "O Lord, what has happened to me is so far behind what You encountered when on this earth." The Lord Jesus condescended himself to come from the highest to the lowest, whereas we today have neither come from the highest nor gone to the lowest. So that we would say, "O Lord, we are far behind You." Let us learn to accept all which legitimately restrains the body. Some people have not disciplined their body for so long that they need to spend more time in training. Hopefully, they will be brought into the work of God within the shortest possible period. If, though, this problem is not resolved or overcome, they will not be able to do His work. One who has not buffeted and subdued his body will quit soon after he joins the race.

Let us keep in mind that gospel work and other service to the Lord is like running a race. Without regular training by which to tame the body, we will not be able to run when God makes extra demands upon us. Running a race implies an additional demand placed upon the body. We cannot afford to allow the latter to remain unbridled. All who are greatly used by God are not only people under God's control but also people of self-control. If we do not have control over our earthly tent, we will certainly fall when a special demand comes upon us. Let it be known and acknowledged as a fact that all particularly valuable works of God are performed within the circumstances of special demand. Of what avail are we if we cannot work under such additional demand? Let us not be careless or undisciplined; rather, let us control the body strictly. If the latter be true of us, then we can forego sleeping, eating and comfort and keep right on working if such special requirements are placed upon our body; for the latter listens to us. As we go forth to work with this body, we make it obey us in spite of sickness or pain. "See with how large letters I write unto you with mine own hand," said Paul. He went and did beyond what he normally could do. Just here we touch the spirit of our brother Paul who forced himself to do the impossible. And this is the very way the spirit of God's servants has always launched them forth throughout the centuries.

If a servant of the Lord, who in ordinary days is healthy and lives comfortably with adequate sleep and nutrition, cannot exercise authority over his body in time of need, he is useless to God. "I buffet my body, and bring it into bondage," Paul declared, " lest by any means, after that I have preached to others, I myself should be rejected [disqualified]" (1 Cor. 9.27). In other words, he was fearful that, having preached the gospel to others, he himself should fail to receive the reward of hearing the Lord say, "Good and well-done, My servant."

We must take this matter to heart, that people who

love their own selves so much that they are undisciplined and untrained cannot serve God. If we really desire to serve Him, we must train ourselves and exercise control over our bodies. And if there is in us a strong love for the Lord, then the body cannot but listen to us: because of the strength of the spirit, the flesh cannot be weak. For the sake of the power of the resurrection life within us, this mortal body must be quickened. We should be brought to the place where it cannot hinder us but, rather, hearken to us. Only in this way may we do the work of the Lord well.

5 | Be Diligent and Not Slothful

The personal life of a worker for God is often determinative of his work. On this pathway of divine service we see a number of young brothers being raised up and made quite useful. From the outset they cause you to feel that here are some good seeds that will eventually blossom forth and bear fruit. But we also see some others who are very self-conceited and self-reliant, and within not too many days thereafter they fall by the wayside. They are not only useless, they in addition greatly disgrace the name of the Lord. For the path they take is so broad that it could not be any broader. Then, too, we see some more people who at the beginning do not show any great promise, but towards the end they manifest more and more their value to God.

You may wish to know what explains all this. We would frankly answer that everyone who would be used by God possesses some fundamental features in constitution and character. And with these fundamental characteristics he may become useful; without them, he will be useless in the pathway of service. A person may be good in many other respects, but if he lacks these basic features of which we have been speaking, he is unable to perform a work well even though he may have the heart to serve. We have never witnessed a worker who, having no control over his body, ever does the work of God. We do not know how this lack may affect other endeavors, but on the pathway of God's service we have never seen it work. Neither have we seen any person who, not capable of listening, is able to serve God. All who would serve the Lord must possess these and other basic characteristics. God in His mercy encourages them and builds them up in these fundamental features of constitution and character so as to enable them to serve well.

Serving God is not so simple a matter. The outward man needs to be broken, as well as to be built up. If you as a person are unfit, that is to say, if you are careless and indulgent in many things, you will not be able to do the work of God. Many are unable to serve well, not because they are lacking in technique or knowledge but because they have one or more problems in their personal character. The failure of many is to be found right here. Hence we must learn to let God deal with us thoroughly in many areas of our lives. Let us never despise the cultivation of these positive basic character traits. Without our permitting the Holy Spirit to transform our character, it can be anticipated that we shall produce little fruit in our undertakings. None of the training in these basic traits can be overlooked. Let us now look at a further matter pertaining to the character of God's workman — namely, that of our not being slothful but diligent (see Rom. 12.11a).

One

> He that received the one went away and digged in the earth, and hid his lord's money. . . . And he also that had received the one talent came and said, Lord, I knew thee that thou art a hard man, reaping where thou didst not sow, and gathering where thou didst not scatter; and I was afraid, and went away and hid thy talent in the earth: lo, thou hast thine own. But his lord answered and said unto him, Thou wicked and slothful servant, thou knewest that I reap where I sowed not, and gather where I did not scatter; thou oughtest therefore to have put my money to the bankers, and at my coming I should have received back mine own with interest. Take ye away therefore the talent from him, and give it unto him that hath the ten talents. . . . And cast ye out the unprofitable servant into the outer darkness . . . (Matt. 25.18–30)

This passage of Scripture shows us that diligence is also a basic requirement of the Lord's workman. Our Lord Jesus plainly points out to us the two fundamental flaws in the character of this servant: one, that he is "wicked," and the other, that he is "slothful." He is wicked because he accuses his lord of being a hard man, reaping where he has not sowed and gathering where he has not scattered. The other flaw about this servant is that he is slothful. When he buries the talent in the earth, what his heart meditates is "wicked," but what his hand does is "slothful." He imagines in his heart the kind of master his lord is. His thought is evil in content. And in burying the talent in the earth, he does not do what he ought to do. Such action reveals none other trait than that of slothfulness. Let us acknowledge here that laziness constitutes the major problem for many people.

A lazy person will not seek out work to do. Even when he definitely sees work, he still hopes there *is* none! Many Christians seem to adopt this same attitude, wherein a big thing dissolves into a small thing, and a small thing dissolves into no thing — that is to say, nothing!; wherein a large work fades into a little work, and a little work disappears into no work. According to experience, there is but one kind of person useful in the work of God, and that is the diligent person. Lazy people are most despicable. One brother has said that even Satan deems the slothful to be useless.

"The sluggard burieth his hand in the dish, and will not so much as bring it to his mouth again" (Prov. 19.24). A person who is slothful is unwilling to do *any*thing. Why? Because he is afraid of getting tired, even in the matter of feeding himself! His hand is in the dish all right, yet he is too lazy even to bring it back to his mouth with food in it. He must eat, but he even expects someone else to bring the food to his mouth! Without any doubt, there is one class of people in the world who are utterly useless — they are the lazy and slothful. God never uses such a person. Let me ask you, have you ever seen a lazy person serving God well? All who are used of the Lord labor hard in His service. They do not waste their time or their energy. Those who daily and constantly only anticipate rest for themselves do not look like God's servants at all. For His servants do not know how to live indolently; they are always about the business of redeeming their time.

Let us observe the apostles in the New Testament. Are we able to find one lazy bone in the lives of the apostles from Peter to Paul? We cannot find any indolence at all in them. They have no thought of wasting time. They toil diligently and seize every opportunity to serve. Paul wrote: "Preach the word; be urgent in season, out of season; reprove, rebuke, exhort, with all long-suffering and teaching" (2 Tim. 4.2). In season or out of season, God's servants are to preach the word. They are to be diligent both in season and out. God's servants are always industrious.

The first apostles toiled tirelessly. So much so that if you were to try to duplicate the work of Paul today, you would soon discover that even if you were to labor until you were eighty years old you could only accomplish one tenth of his work. Let us look at Paul's work more specifically. How unceasingly he toils! There is not a trace of laziness in him. He is engaged either in preaching the gospel everywhere or in reasoning with people. He is either preaching or writing letters. Even in prison he writes them. And those letters of his which touched the spiritual heights were written from prison. Although he himself was in bonds, the word of God was not bound. Paul was in truth a most diligent person. He was like his Lord, who was never slothful.

In New Testament Greek three different words may be translated "slothful" in English. One is *argos* (meaning: inactive, unprofitable, slow); another is *nōthros* (indolent, sluggish, dull); and a third, *oknēros* (shrinking, irksome). Combining the meanings of these different Greek words, we have the thoughts of "slow," "delaying," "hesitating," "idle" and "irksome." Basically, the meaning comes down to the idea of not running, not working; to the idea of the avoidance of doing many things and of reducing something to nothing.

There was once a joke about a doorkeeper. His duty was to open the door whenever the bell rang. One day someone rang the bell, but he did not open the door. When asked why he did not do so, his answer was, "I hoped he would not ring the bell." How laughable, yet how lamentable! People were ringing the bell, yet he was hoping all along that they would not ring it! What is your opinion of such a person? No doubt not a very commendable one. Yet unfortunately, in God's work, many believers act in the same manner. They expect nothing to come their way, and yet when something in fact does come, they hope that it will be nothing. How thankful they are if there is *really* nothing, so that they will not need to do *anything*. What is this trait? Is it not "slothfulness"?

The central implication of the meaning of slothfulness is to postpone as long as possible or to do as slowly as permissible. One day's work can be dragged out over ten days or even weeks or months. To do a thing sluggishly is to have the trait of slothfulness. This is in fact what Matthew 20.3,6 calls "standing idle" or "standing around"; or what in Philippians 3.1 is termed as being "irksome." In the case of some brothers and sisters, whenever anything is laid upon them, and even so slight a thing, they are of so lazy a disposition that they consider this to be burdensome for them. They sigh deeply as though a heavy load has been placed upon their shoulders. Not so with Paul. It is not an easy thing for this apostle to write from prison under a most difficult environment, but as he writes the letter to the Philippians, he exhorts the brethren, saying, "Rejoice in the Lord always: again I will say, Rejoice" (4.4). Circumstantially speaking, he is in deep affliction; nonetheless, he says this: "To write the same things to you, to me indeed is not irksome" (3.1b). He is not slothful; on the contrary, he considers nothing too hard and does not know what laziness is. We learn from studying Paul's life that people used of God are full of zeal, knowing neither idleness nor weariness.

Many brethren are of little usefulness in the service of God because they dislike work. They look for less work, and if they can, they will not work at all. They lack the character of diligence. To tell the truth, not only must we say that the slothful cannot be *God's* servants, they cannot even be *man's*. Many are disqualified as servants of God due to their laziness. They exalt themselves as so-called "servants of God," acting as though they are beyond the direction of any man. None can exercise any control over them for they deem themselves to be *God's* servants. Yet suppose their master is changed from God to someone else; it will then be that their worthlessness shall at once be manifested. For no earthly master would allow them to be so careless in managing his business. For this reason, our disposition must be exercised to such a degree that not only are we not bothered in serving but we even delight to serve. We will joyfully spend and be spent for the children of God. We love to be engaged in working. On the other hand, the lack of such a disposition makes us unfit to be the Lord's servants. "These hands," Paul once declared, "ministered unto my necessities, and to them that were with me" (Acts 20.34). Those two hands of his were so beautiful because they worked day and night without the slightest sign of slothfulness. Now it is such people as Paul who are truly the servants of God!

Two

What is diligence? Diligence is a not being slothful, that is to say, a not being afraid to work. It is not hoping that things might go away but, rather, *seeking* for things to do. We should be aware that in the service of God, if we do not look for work to do, the result will be that we shall indeed be able to rest for a day or two. In the Lord's service, we must not be people who work only when it *comes* to us. Such an attitude reveals our sluggishness. A diligent person is never idle; he is continually searching for work to do. He is always studying, praying, waiting, and considering what service he can render. If we do only what comes our way, we shall soon find that there is less and less coming our way to do. In order to serve God, let us try to discover works to perform. Let us pray and wait more before the Lord. Let us be on the alert to find more and more works to do. This is the way of service. "My Father worketh even until now," observed the Lord Jesus, "and I work" (John 5.12). We must not change this into: "My Father *resteth* even until now, and I *rest*." Slothfulness is the one sure way to effect such a change.

Yet our way must always be: "My Father *worketh* even until now, and I *work*."

In the light of all this, then, let us ask God: "O God, what do You want me to do?" Let us note that after His conversation with the Samaritan woman, Jesus spoke a very special word: "Say not ye, There are yet four months and then cometh the harvest? behold, I say unto you, Lift up your eyes, and look on the fields, that they are white already unto harvest" (John 4.35). According to the disciples' estimate, the harvest had to wait for four more months; but according to the Lord's appraisal, the harvest is now.

Today we are in need of people who can lift up their eyes and see that the harvest is ready. The lack of such vision postpones the harvest to four months later. Many simply hide at home and do not travel on the path of God. Many eyes are not looking out at what God is doing today. In the preceding verse of the passage that recounts this incident in John 4, we find that the Lord Jesus told the disciples, "My meat is to do the will of him that sent me, and to accomplish his work" (v.34). This teaches us, does it not, how frequently we need to lift up our eyes and *look*. There will be no work if we do not do so.

Accordingly, this matter of service is really one of diligence, of not being slothful. Work is not measured by what is in our hand but by our lifting up the eyes and looking for service to render. God is moving in many ways and in many directions, and if we lift up our eyes we will discover them. You and I should lift up our eyes and look to see if there is any harvest and if the harvest is white. By searching and looking, we will in fact find works to do. How surprising that many stand idle as though there is no work to do!

He who likes to work seeks for it, but he who dislikes work avoids it. The diligent, as soon as he is out of work, will wait before God for new work to do. He always searches for opportunities. Once a brother said, "So many brothers come from abroad, and yet brother so-and-so has not spent any time in fellowshiping with them. This is really outrageous." "Why do you not tell him?" asked another brother. "Do I need to tell him?" answered the first brother. His answer is absolutely correct. A person who serves the Lord ought before God to seek out work to do and fellowship to render. This, however, should not be construed to mean that one should intentionally keep himself unduly busy with so many things. It simply suggests that a servant of the Lord ought to seek God and habitually lift up his eyes and look. If a person is truly occupied, God will not place extra burdens upon him. But when he has time to spare, then he should ask the Lord, "Lord, what do You want me to do?" Merely by lifting up his eyes, he shall see that many people need his service.

There is but one explanation for the fact that a person has nothing to do—which is, that he is normally slothful, that he is a lazy person. He cannot finish a job in ten days which others might do in one day. He has no desire to serve. We ought all to seek actively for work to do. If we do not search and pray before God to find service to render, we are undoubtedly slothful individuals. It is certain that even after five or ten years we will still be able to do very little.

In performing the Lord's service, a basic requirement is that of clear vision before God. As soon as a work appears, we know this should be done. If our eyes are veiled, how can we possibly see any service to perform? Our spirit needs to be sensitive to God; otherwise, we shall labor rather sluggishly. We must pay attention to our Lord's command: "Lift up your eyes, and look." Do not rely on what other people may say: "There are yet four months, and then cometh the harvest." Listen to the word of the Lord: "Lift up your eyes, and look on the fields, that they are white already unto harvest." How strange it is that we pass by the fields daily and yet our eyes never see the harvest, we thinking it will come four months later. Though our hands have already come near to what needs to be done, we are nonetheless unaware of it. This is indeed astonishing.

We have never seen anyone used of God who was slothful. The person whom God can use is one who seeks for work to do and who is willing to exert himself. He does not dare to waste time by fulfilling one day's work in two days. Anyone who is careless about time is not of much use in God's hand. How many people wait to be pushed, just as a pendulum clock needs a flick of the hand to be started. Push, and these people move; otherwise they stay put. Such people are unprofitable in God's service. Whenever there are brethren who are diligently laboring, there is result. In some places God is doing a great work because there are many who are toiling untiringly; whereas in other localities, the work of God is withering because many are idling about: the work there is poor because the people are slothful.

One form of the noun "diligence" in Greek is *spoudē*, a term which denotes earnestness, zeal (or sometimes the haste accompanying this—as in Mark 6.25 and Luke 1.39, where *spoudē* is translated "haste" in both the AV and RV); in Romans 12.8 it is translated "diligence" in both Bible versions; in Romans 12.11, it is translated "business" in the AV ("diligence" in the RV); in 2 Corinthians 8.7, it is translated "diligence" in the AV ("earnestness" in the RV); in Hebrews 6.11, 2 Peter 1.5 and Jude 3, both versions have "diligence"; and in 2 Corinthians 7.11 and 12, it is translated, respectively, "carefulness" and "care" in the AV ("earnest care" in both verses in the RV). The complementary verb form is *spoudazō*, which signifies to hasten to do a thing, to exert oneself, endeavor, or give diligence. Thus we are given the understanding of its manifold meaning. In Romans 12.11, the translated words "diligence" and "slothful" are put together in the RV (or ASV), the result of which is: "in diligence not slothful"—where the word diligence is used synonymously with endeavor or business, which is thus to say, that one should not be slothful or lazy in one's endeavors, affairs or business. *

In other words, our not being diligent is to be slothful. In spiritual matters, one person may have to do the labor of ten or even a hundred people. How can

---

*The author based the entire paragraph above on W. E. Vine, *An Expository Dictionary of New Testament Words* (first published in London, 1940 in four separate vols., but since then has been available in one bound vol.). See 17th Impression (Old Tappan, N.J.: Fleming H. Revell Co., 1966), I, p.311 ("Diligence") and p.160 ("Business"). Please note that Vine's use of the abbreviation RV

we ever meet the demands of the work if we are lazy people and need ten persons to do the work of one?

We must have this disposition of diligence. Whether we are in fact busily engaged is actually of secondary consideration; what is of *primary* importance is our having a diligent *disposition*. Before God, we ought to be those who diligently seek out work to do. This is not meant to imply, of course, that we must keep ourselves in a constant state of hustle and bustle, for that can only encumber us. To be diligent simply means not to be fearful of work but to serve God zealously, always being fervent in spirit. Find work to do before God. This may not necessarily be manifested in action, but it certainly must be present in our disposition or character. In case our disposition is one of slothfulness, then we may indeed be busy for twelve hours in a single day, but we will not last long; for only those whose disposition is diligent and not slothful can alone be useful.

A person who is constitutionally lazy and indolent may in truth force himself to work for two hours, yet he prays from morning till night that a big thing will dissolve into a small thing, and that a small thing will fade into no thing so that he can end up not having to do anything. Not so, though, with our Lord Jesus,

---

above has reference to both the English Revised Version of 1885 and the American Revised Version (the latter being the same as the American Standard Version of 1901—the version, of course, used throughout this present volume unless otherwise indicated). AV is the abbreviation, of course, for the Authorized or King James Version of 1611.—*Translator*

because He came to the world to seek out men and to find work to accomplish. Said the Lord: "the Son of man came to seek and to save that which was lost" (Luke 19.10). He did not come just to *meet* men, He came to *seek* them. Only a disposition such as this can enable us to walk in the way of God.

> Yea, and for this very cause adding on your part all diligence, in your faith supply virtue; and in your virtue knowledge; and in your knowledge self-control; and in your self-control patience; and in your patience godliness; and in your godliness brotherly kindness; and in your brotherly kindness love. (2 Peter 1.5–7)

All this is termed *diligence*! Peter mentioned here the sevenfold "adding" or "supplying." A diligent person is always in the process of adding, he never stops short. Oh that we might cultivate such a habit before God! Having *this* one, let us add *another* one, and another, and another . . . Let us be adding on *all* the time. For such pursuit before God will most assuredly bring in results. But if our temperament be indolent, we can accomplish nothing anywhere.

A person who has no sense of responsibility, no burden upon his shoulder, who has no desire to develop the work or to do it well, who has no thought of gaining more people for God, and no interest in spreading the gospel to the ends of the earth, is most liable to let all things slip by. How can God ever use such a man? How can he possibly work for God if he is not moved when he meets an unsaved soul? The workman whom God desires is one who will not let go. He is always adding on — one after another — the features of Christian character. And "if these things are yours and abound," concluded Peter, "they make you to be not idle nor unfruitful unto the knowledge of our Lord Jesus Christ" (v.8). Hence Peter told us here to abound in diligence.

Yet how is this done? By adding on one thing after another; and the consequence is that we will not be idle. In other words, slothfulness must be dealt with by diligence. In diligence, one thing is added to another. There is never a sense of self-contentment, nor the thought of quitting, but a keeping on until one abounds in the knowledge of the Lord Jesus Christ to the end that we be neither idle nor unfruitful. We need to exercise ourselves in these "addings" continually so as to deal with the natural tendency in us toward slothfulness.

Let us pay attention to Peter's words here. If we were preaching on diligence, we might say let us diligently add this to that and then stop. But the apostle keeps on adding a total of seven times. He shows us how, having obtained one, we must add another and another and another until we abound in these facets of Christian character so that we are neither idle nor unfruitful. May we ask God to transform our character, causing us to be those who delight in work, who seek opportunity to serve, and who are not slothful or indolent people.

Yet let us note further that Peter did not stop even here. He continued on, declaring: "Yea, I will give diligence that at every time ye may be able after my decease to call these things to remembrance" (v.15). The apostle would give diligence to put them in remembrance. Perhaps he saw too many lazy people; hence he wanted to use diligence himself to call them to remember these things. Oh, let us learn to serve God diligently and swiftly. Let us seize every opportunity to serve. Besides working with our hands and feet, we must also have an attitude of heart that is bent towards work. Those who know the truth most clearly before the Lord but who are constitutionally lazy are absolutely useless and cannot serve God.

Both the second letter to Timothy and the one to Titus mention something concerning service responsibility. "Give diligence to come shortly unto me" (2 Tim. 4.9). If a person is diligent, he will come quickly; if he is slothful he will come slowly, or perhaps even not at all. Paul said it again, just twelve verses later: "Give diligence to come before winter" (4.21a). And Paul also wrote to Titus in the same vein: "Give diligence to come unto me to Nicopolis" (Titus 3.12a). The word "diligence" is used in all these instances, thus placing some emphasis on this matter in these letters.

The Epistle of Jude employs the same word: "Beloved, while I was giving all diligence to write unto you of our common salvation, I was constrained to write unto you exhorting you to contend earnestly for the faith which was once for all delivered unto the saints." (v.3).

In another place Paul mentioned diligence once more. In 2 Corinthians 7, in speaking about their repentance, he wrote, "For behold, this selfsame thing, that ye were made sorry after a godly sort, what earnest care [in Greek, this is the same noun *(spoudē)* used elsewhere for "diligence"] it wrought in you . . ." (v.11).

A person who truly desires to serve the Lord ought to sense the greatness of his responsibility, the urgency

of outside needs, as well as the shortness of his time
and the limitedness of his lifespan. If we have this kind
of consciousness we will be diligent and not slothful.
The lack of such an awareness will make us unfruitful
in God's work. This burden of the work of the Lord
should press us to such a point that we have to work,
even at times foregoing eating, sleeping and rest, thus
finding the right path in God's service. Otherwise, if
we consider rest as our basic and most essential requirement of life, we will not be able to accomplish anything
in the work of God.

Let us understand that our time cannot be shorter,
our responsibility cannot be greater, and the outside
needs cannot be more urgent. It must be as though we
are dying people preaching the gospel to a dying world,
as though our breath will soon expire and opportunity
will quickly pass. Here we must give our all. How can
we possibly accomplish anything if we are sluggish in
seeing outside needs and indifferent to our responsibility
and limited time? Today, every servant of God must
serve with a sense that he is a dying person with a
limited time span. How, then, can anyone be slothful
amidst such circumstances?

Accordingly, let us rise up today and learn to drive
ourselves to be diligent people—even as Paul said, "I
buffet my body, and bring it into bondage." It is not
enough merely to have a desire to serve God. We must
realize that unless we beat ourselves to the degree that
we cannot fail to give our all daily before God, then
we can neither work nor be useful. We should not
deceive ourselves. One may say to the Lord, "I am willing to sacrifice my life to You," and yet he is habitually

lazy: his temperament is to avoid doing things. By bringing such a bad habit into the Lord's work, he will let the work of the Lord go! Had Paul waited till he had received the call of the Macedonian in a vision before setting to work, then what the book of Acts would have recorded of his labors would have been merely that single work in Macedonia; for out of all the labors he performed, the Macedonian call came but once. All his other works had been accomplished through his burdens before God.

If you wait until you are sought by the brethren, you will be of little use in your life. Work comes through I myself taking up a burden. I am one who realizes that the time is short, the outside need is great, and the work of Satan is rampant. And hence I cannot but be diligent and I cannot rest.

Three

Let us return to the passage in Matthew 25.18–30 and review again what are its implications for us who would serve the Lord as His workmen. In the future when we are before the judgment-seat of Christ, two charges may possibly be leveled at us: one is of our having been wicked, the other, of our having been slothful. What is meant by being wicked? It is considering the Lord to be hard. Perhaps not many will have been guilty of this sin of wickedness. But I fear that nine out of every ten who shall one day stand before the Lord will have to confess that they had been slothful. At that time, the Lord will say, "Cast ye out the unprofitable servant into the outer darkness!" (see v.30a) The Lord judges the slothful as an unprofitable servant.

Sometimes we may question why God uses a certain brother. We will be shown that it was because he gave his all. He spent many hours and was involved day and night. The path before us of service to the Lord lies in the way of diligence—a way that is untrod by the slothful. We are required to put our all into the work. Unless we solve the problem of our lazy character, we can do nothing. Through indolence a person is reduced into half a person or even less: he later may become only one tenth of a man. Today, few really know God. How can His work be done if things are dragged out over a lengthy period instead of being quickly finished? In the past we have witnessed many to have fallen by the wayside and become useless because they were slothful people. These ought to be a warning to us. Today we need to change our habit and have our character transformed. May God eliminate this slothfulness from among us and may we strictly cause our body to listen to us. Otherwise, there is no way through for the work of God.

How prevalent is this problem of laziness in the work of God. Possibly nine out of ten are of this temperament. A person who serves the Lord needs to have the kind of drive within which keeps him going. And hence the Scriptures do not employ a horse but an ox to signify service, for the work of an ox is steady. Today, tomorrow and the day after it works steadily with no let up. How can you expect any result if today you have the mood to work and tomorrow you have no mood to work—if today you work because the weather is good and tomorrow you quit because the weather is bad? But if step by step you labor on, day after day, always working, never letting up, you are bound to have results. May God deliver us from much frivolity and from much foolishness. May He cause us to be like an ox, so that in the service of God we will take up, hold fast, press on and not let up. We shall be diligent and not slothful; and thus we may find our way in God's service.

In the Old Testament, the book of Proverbs speaks the most definitely and frequently on slothfulness. The Hebrew word *atsel* is translated "slothful" or "sluggard" fourteen times (6.6,9; 10.26; 13.4; 15.19; 19.24; 20.4; 21.25; 22.13; 24.30; 26.13,14,15,16); the Hebrew word *atslah*, translated "slothfulness," is used once (19.15); and the Hebrew word *remiyyah*, translated "slothful," is used twice (12.24,27). So we see that Solomon spoke often on this matter.

Let us clearly understand that slothfulness is a habit which is developed over a long period of time. It cannot be changed within just a day or two. Except we deal drastically with this habit, we shall find ourselves entangled by it throughout our lives. Let us not think that by merely listening to a message we will be able to resolve it. It is not that simple. Know and understand that it had become a disposition over many years of developed habit in our life; and it can therefore only be changed by means of severe discipline over perhaps a long period of time before God. Hence let all who are habitually lazy deal with this matter unrelentingly. Without such treatment no slothful person shall be able to do well for the Lord since he is constitutionally indisposed to working. There is no hope for such undealt-with people in the work of God.

On the other hand all who are truly God's servants are "busybodies," for they find troubles for themselves. They put themselves under burdens; they seek out solutions for problems; they do not evade difficulties. So let those of us who desire to serve the Lord deal severely with the habit of fearing troubles and evading responsibilities. We must strictly deal with this area of our lives because the slothful cannot serve God.

6 | Restrained in Speech

One

Many people should be greatly used by God; they should be powerful vessels in His hand. Yet they fail to be used by God; and even if they are used, they are not very effective vessels. One of the prime reasons is their lack of restraint in speech. Carelessness in this matter of speech is an opening through which the power of God may either flow out or leak away. Our speech may serve as either an outlet for God's power or as an escape hole for power to leak away. Unfortunately, many allow the power of God to leak away.

James wrote in his letter as follows: "Doth the fountain send forth from the same opening sweet water and bitter?" (3.11) The mouth of God's workman ought to issue forth sweet and living water. He should proclaim the word of God. We cannot, for example, use the same bucket to carry water for cooking and water for sewage. Were the same bucket used for both, it would endanger human health, even human life. In similar manner, if our mouth is used to proclaim the word of God, then we must not use it casually for other purposes. If we use this mouth of ours to speak of many things other than God's word, we will not be qualified to proclaim His word. Many are not used, or are used limitedly, by God because out of their mouths issue forth two opposite kinds of things — the bitter as well as the sweet. Their mouths utter many words not of God as well as the word of God itself.

We ought to realize before the Lord that our mouth has been offered to proclaim His word. Is it not a tremendous responsibility to have God's word spoken through us? It is recorded in Numbers 16 that Korah and his co-conspirators verbally attacked Moses and Aaron. They then brought their censers to God. But they had sinned and so they perished. Yet these censers were holy. So God spoke to Moses and instructed him as follows: ". . . take up the censers out of the burning, and scatter thou the fire yonder; for they are holy . . .; and let them be made beaten plates for a covering of the altar" (Num. 16.37–38). Whatever has once been offered to the Lord is forever holy, and must therefore not be used for another purpose.

Some brothers and sisters incorrectly entertain the notion that they can speak the word of God at one time and the word of Satan at another (the lie, for instance, is, as we know, of Satan). But this we must not do. Once a believer's mouth proclaims the word of God, that mouth is forever the Lord's. Sadly, the power of many believers has leaked away through their speech. Some brothers have the potential of being greatly used of the

Lord, but they utter many words not of God, and consequently their inner power leaks out while they are speaking. Keep well in mind that a fountain can send forth only one kind of water. Once your mouth announces the word of God, you need to realize that henceforth you have no authority to say what is not of God. Your mouth is sanctified; it is holy. Anything which has once been consecrated is forever the Lord's. It ought not to be taken back. Thus we are shown the relationship between the Lord's word and our word. Your mouth is sanctified and you can only speak God's word.

What a pity that many who ought to be used by God are disabled because their mouth is as a large hole that leaks out His power. Power is drained if our mouth sends forth two kinds of speech. The problem of many lies in their much speaking, as the Preacher of old makes clear: "a dream cometh with a multitude of business, and a fool's voice with a multitude of words" (Eccl. 5.3). Due to their multitude of words, the power of many people is sapped. They like to talk about many things; they always have something to speak about. They not only talk a lot, they also love to spread words spoken by other people. Oh! do let us keep and guard our mouth as carefully as we ought to keep and guard our heart (see Prov. 4.23) — especially for those of us who are to serve as God's mouthpiece, who are to be used of Him to proclaim His word. Our mouth is sanctified as a holy vessel for the service of the Lord. How much more, then, must we keep it as we keep our heart! We cannot let it be unbridled.

Two

A servant of God needs to be attentive to quite a number of things (twelve, in fact) with regard to speech:

First, we need to be careful before God concerning the words which we frequently hear. For what we usually listen to demonstrates the kind of people we are. Many will not tell you their affairs because they know you are not their kind of person, and therefore it is futile to tell you anyway. But if people continue to relate to you a certain sort of words with ease, it is because they know you are of their kind, and by relating them to you they are sure of the effect. Therefore, the kind of words that can be piled upon you only confirms the kind of person you are.

Second, the type of words we easily believe substantiates a similar kind of character in us. For a certain type of person will believe a certain type of words. To hear wrongly and to believe readily is due to dimness of sight — that is to say, it is a case of not being in the light of God. The lack of light creates the error. Consequently, the type of words we *hear* oftentimes reveals our weakness. But then, too, *believing* a certain type of words also unveils our spiritual ailment. Sometimes people believe before the words are even heard. They rejoice when the words finally *do* come. However strange these utterances may be, they take them as trustworthy. So that the type of words one believes shows the kind of person he is.

Third, there is another feature which bears the same

nature as that of hearing and believing, and that is, the *spreading* of words. Having heard and believed a certain sort of words, one spreads these same words around. This indicates not only the kind of person he is and the lack of light in him, but it also betrays his desire of involving others in doing the same. Listening is hearing what another says; believing is taking in what is said; but the act of spreading is getting oneself fully involved. Many so love to talk about and spread around all kinds of things that whatever power they have leaks away altogether. With the result that they are not capable of being good ministers of God's word.

Fourth, speaking inaccurately is another serious facet to this matter of speech. Some may have a different problem than the aforementioned characteristics: their speech is frequently inexact. They will say one thing at one time and say another at another time. A person with a double tongue is not qualified to be a deacon (see 1 Tim. 3.8), for he will speak according to the people he meets. He will say one thing to the face and another thing behind the back. Such a person is useless in the work of God. If we are unable to bridle our tongue, how can we control ourselves and serve God? We must discipline ourselves and bring this member of our body into subjection before we can ever serve the Lord well. For as the Scriptures have told us, the tongue is the most corrupted member in our body and which often leads us into the most terrible of troubles. Speaking inaccurately, speaking with a double tongue, and speaking dishonestly—these all reveal a weak character. Such kind of people cannot stand before God, and they have no power with Him. To be careless and shifty in speech is a serious breach of good character. It needs to be dealt with, lest it greatly affect the Lord's work.

Fifth, speaking deliberately with a double tongue. This is more serious than the *ignorant* double tongue discussed above. Some may be double-tongued due to ignorance. They speak in such a way because they are so naïve as to see little difference between "yea" and "nay." To them there is no "yea" or "nay"; everything is fuzzy. When they are asked if a thing is black, they will say it is black; but when asked if the same thing is white, their answer will be that it is white. For them, everything is gray. They are rather careless and thoughtless. Such kind of double-tongued speech is due to ignorance.

But others are *deliberately* double-tongued: they speak with purpose. Now for such people as this it is not just a weak temperament, it is a moral corruption. We are told in Matthew 21.23–27 that when the chief priests and the elders of the people came to the Lord Jesus and asked Him, "By what authority doest thou these things?", He answered by asking them, "The baptism of John, whence was it? from heaven or from men?" They reasoned among themselves, saying, "If we shall say, From heaven; he will say unto us, Why then did ye not believe him? But if we shall say, From men; we fear the multitude; for all hold John as a prophet." So they answered the Lord Jesus by saying, "We know not." Such an answer is a *willful* deception.

Yet let us recall what our Lord said: "let your speech

be, Yea, yea; Nay, nay: and whatsoever is more than these is of the evil one" (Matt. 5.37). To say yea, yea, and nay, nay — this is honest and open speech. If I inwardly reason as to how people will respond to what I say, I am engaged in manipulation. This ought not to be the intention and attitude of one who seeks to do the work of the Lord. If I speak with craftiness, my speech becomes an instrument of deceit! We, however, would rather imitate our Lord, who refused to speak when people tried to accuse Him by attempting to catch Him in His word (see John 8.5–6). If we must speak, let it be yea, yea and nay, nay. For whatever is more than these, said Jesus, is of the evil one. The clever, therefore, are lost here.

Paul persuaded the Corinthians, saying: "Let no man deceive himself. If any man thinketh that he is wise among you in this world, let him become a fool, that he may become wise" (1 Cor. 3.18). Again, he wrote to the Romans: "I would have you wise unto that which is good, and simple unto that which is evil" (Rom. 16.19c). Paul asserted these things because cleverness in these matters is unacceptable to God. Our wisdom is in the Lord's hand. We must not be double-tongued.

How sad that this is a problem with many believers. Those whose words are not trustworthy are of no use in the hand of God. Sooner or later they will spoil His work. How can they be used by Him if they all the time vacillate between yea and nay, right and wrong, can do and cannot do? Those whose speech is ever changing and never dependable are useless in the work of God.

Sixth, our very hearing must be dealt with. We who

are God's workmen have, for that very reason, much more contact with people, and thus many more opportunities than others both to speak and hear. If we are not disciplined in our speech, we may easily preach the word of God on the one hand but sow seeds of discord on the other. Without restraint in speech we will be building up the work of God on the one hand while tearing it down on the other. Hence we need the restraint of God in our very hearing of things. Many times when brothers and sisters are telling us of their affairs which may relate both to their personal need and to the work of God, we must of course try our best to listen. We must be people who can indeed listen, find out the problems or difficulties involved, and render whatever help is required. But *while* listening, and immediately upon understanding the situation, you must stop listening. You can kindly tell the person: "This that you have said is enough, you may stop now." It would not be right for you to continue listening out of curiosity, as though you were about the business of listening to stories. What the person has thus far spoken is quite ample for you to now know where the problem lies. As soon as you have grasped the situation by means of the adequate knowledge he has related to you, you can say to him, "Brother, this is enough."

We must not have the lust of endlessly listening. We as human beings do have the inordinate desire of wanting to know things, and thus the lust of wishing to hear things. But there must be a proper limit to our knowing and hearing. And as that limit or measure is reached, let us not continue to pursue that line any longer. We only listen in order to pray. We only hear for the sake of solving problems which our brothers and sisters may have personally or that relate to God's work. Therefore, we must cease our listening at a certain point without the slightest hesitation.

Seventh, the need for learning to be trustworthy. When a person shares with you his problem, that is because he has confidence in you. You must therefore not betray his confidence by carelessly spreading shared matters abroad. Except for whatever necessity there may be to do so in the work, you should never talk about those matters. How can you possibly be involved in the Lord's work if you exercise no restraint in speech? A servant of God is entrusted with many things. He ought to see that his trust is holy and worthy. The words spoken to you are not your property; these become instead matters of your ministry and service. Consequently, you must not gossip with those words spoken to you in confidence.

In spiritual matters we must learn to keep and protect our brothers and sisters by not casually mentioning their spiritual difficulties. It is admittedly an entirely different situation if there is a need to talk about these difficulties in order to discharge our responsibility in the work of God and solve them. Nevertheless, much speaking is a great loss, even at times an irreparable loss. One who speaks too much and gossips a great deal cannot be trusted in the Lord's work. Let us be warned before God; let us ask Him to restrain our speech lest we thoughtlessly open our mouth. Whether or not a person has truly achieved self-control becomes *most* evident by his speech. If he is disciplined, his speech is with restraint. This is something to which we must pay very close attention.

Eighth, there is the necessity to take heed concerning lies. A double tongue easily leads to lying. Words which are spoken to mislead people to arrive at false conclusions are lies; likewise, words which are uttered to intentionally create wrong concepts are lies as well. Sometimes, there may not be any false statement in the words spoken; they are nonetheless spoken with such craftiness that they produce a wrong impression. This too is a lie. Hence let us understand that the honesty of our speech must be judged by our inward intention as well as by our outward words. If a brother asks you something which you cannot tell, it is far better for you to say, "I cannot tell," than to deceive him. A false statement is a lie; yet a misleading speech is also a lie. If we want people to believe in truthful things, we must not mislead them to believe in falsehood. With respect to God's children, their speech must be "Yea, yea" and "Nay, nay"; whatever goes beyond that "is of the evil one."

On one occasion the Lord Jesus spoke the following strong words to the Jews: "Ye are of your father the devil, and the lusts of your father it is your will to do. ... When he speaketh a lie, he speaketh of his own: for he is a liar, and the father thereof" (John 8.44). Lying comes from the devil, he who has lied from the very beginning to the present moment. He is a liar; yet not only he lies himself but also he is the father of all other liars. For this reason, it is detestable to find a lie in the mouth of a child of God, especially on the lips of a workman of the Lord. How far one has surely fallen from grace if he has engaged in lying. It is a serious breach of our Christian constitution. It is a most solemn matter!

We must guard ourselves against lying. We dare not say that our speech is altogether correct, since the more we take heed to our speech the more we sense its difficulty. Sometimes we want to speak truthfully, yet through a slight inadvertence we speak inaccurately. If we find it hard to speak precisely while we *are* on our guard, how much more inexact will our speech be if we are *not* on our guard! If it is not easy to speak truthfully under control, what shall our speech be if we do not exercise control at all? Thus we must control ourselves and take heed to our speech. We must not be lax in our discipline lest we are disqualified from serving God. For the Lord cannot use anyone who speaks both for Him as well as for Satan. God will never use such a person.

Ninth, there is another point that requires our special attention, which is, we must "not strive nor cry aloud." It was prophesied concerning the earthly life of our Lord Jesus that He would "not strive, nor cry aloud; neither [would] any one hear his voice in the streets" (Matt. 12.19). The apostle Paul wrote in a similar vein: "The Lord's servant must not strive" (2 Tim. 2.24a). No servant of God may strive or clamor. Clamoring is unseemly. The Lord's servant ought to so discipline himself that he will "not strive nor cry aloud." Crying aloud is a token of less power. It is at least an indication of having less control over oneself. As a servant of the Lord a person ought not to raise his voice so loud as to be heard by people in the next room. Our Lord Jesus has set for us an example in His not ever having had His voice heard in the streets. Such restraint is more than speaking no lie. Though our speech may be true and exact, we will neither strive nor clamor. Should a brother or a sister shout aloud, we who are self-disciplined will nonetheless keep silent on matters. We will control ourselves and control our voice even as our Lord Jesus did. Let us learn before God to bridle our mouth that we may not make noise or strive impetuously. This does not mean, however, that hereafter we must put on a stern face and tightly clamp our lips shut whenever we meet people. No, no; we need to be natural and converse naturally with people. Yet we shall have many difficulties in the work if we do not control our voice. We hope that all who serve the Lord will be more sensitive and tender and polite. Look at our Lord Jesus. How sensitive and tender He was while on earth. He neither strove nor cried aloud, nor was His voice heard in the streets. God's servant ought to impress people as being a tender person.

Tenth, let us watch intention and inward fact. Outward speech is one thing; intention of the heart is quite another. God's children should not observe the exactness of their speech but simultaneously neglect the accuracy of the inward fact of the heart. We would stress the latter over the former. Many have the weakness of watching the correctness of their words but overlooking the truthfulness of inward fact. Let us see that even if we speak carefully and accurately, we may nonetheless be untrustworthy. For in the presence of God we must be even more attentive to the preciseness of inward fact. We will be of little use to God if our speech is exact but the inward fact be distorted.

Some brothers and sisters are most careful in speech, but we still cannot trust them. Though we are not able to discover any fault in their words, we still sense that they seek the accuracy of speech rather than that of fact as well. Suppose, for example, you hate a brother. This is an inward fact. According to fact, you hate him in your heart. But when you meet him on the street, you still nod at him and shake hands with him. You even entertain him when he comes to your house. You visit him during his sickness and send money and clothes to him in his time of need. But one day when you are asked about your attitude towards that brother, you may quite correctly answer as follows (though in fact you hate him in your heart): "Did I not nod at him and shake his hand? Did I not visit him during his sickness and take care of him in his need?" Truly, reason is on your side. You are right before God's law and correct in your speech. Nevertheless, this that you have conveyed by your correct speech is nonetheless a lie, because the inward fact disagrees.

We know some brothers and sisters who lay much stress on procedure. You cannot find any fault with them in this regard. Yet their heart is at odds with their procedure. There is nothing wrong in what they say, but they do not mean what they say. This is to be condemned. When you open your mouth to talk, do you only watch the correctness of procedure as evidence of your truthfulness? If so, you need to examine before

God the intention of your heart. For this is a basic problem behind much of man's speech. It is not enough merely to be correct in words; nor is it even enough to treat others well. These things cannot be put forward as proofs that you do not hate another person. We must look at the inward fact—the true state of the heart—and not only at the words of our mouth. To speak truthfully, we must have true fact inside. If outward speech does not bear out the inward fact, then what is said is nothing but a lie. How sad that many live under this kind of illusion. Hence in our speech we must watch not only our words but even more deeply, our intention.

Eleventh, the matter of speaking no idle words. The Lord has declared that "out of the abundance of the heart the mouth speaketh.... Every idle word that men shall speak, they shall give account thereof in the day of judgment." He then continued with this sobering statement: "For by thy words thou shalt be justified, and by thy words thou shalt be condemned" (Matt. 12.34–37). It is obviously most expedient that God's children not speak idle words when they are gathered together. This is not to suggest, however, that we should refrain from greeting each other or chatting about the weather or the flowers. Such words as these are within the proper bounds of human relationship and are therefore justified. The expression of idle words, though, means something else. It signifies gossiping about a matter that has absolutely no relation to you. It need not at all be done. Yet if people do, then the Lord clearly states that "they shall give account thereof in the day of judgment." An idle word is not spoken only once;

it will at least be spoken twice: today it is uttered, and in the day of judgment it will be repeated once more. Every idle word which men shall speak shall be repeated verbatim in the day of judgment. On that day, you shall discover how many idle words you have spoken, and you will be justified or condemned by your words. None of us can afford to speak carelessly.

We must avoid foolish talking and jesting. Saying a few clever words or telling a few harmless jokes to the little children constitute a different category of speech. No, what we have reference to here is what Paul mentioned in Ephesians: "nor filthiness, nor foolish talking, or jesting" (5.4a). Here Paul had reference to flimsy and flippant words which we must totally reject.

Furthermore, we should not speak derisively. While the Lord was on the cross, all sorts of people mocked and ridiculed Him, saying such things as: "if thou art the Son of God, come down from the cross" (Matt. 27.40b); "He saved others; he himself he cannot save" (v.42a); "let him come down from the cross, and we will believe on him" (v.42b); "He trusteth on God; let him deliver him now, if he desireth him" (v.43a); and, "let us see whether Elijah cometh to take him down" (Mark 15.36b). All this is an example of derision and mocking in its worst form. Those who do not believe in the second coming of the Lord say, mockingly, "Where is the promise of his coming? for, from the day that the fathers fell asleep, all things continue as they were from the beginning of the creation"! (2 Peter 3.4) The world will mock and employ all forms of ridicule; but these do not befit God's children.

Finally, *twelfth,* speaking behind people's back or speaking judgmentally should likewise be avoided. A reviler commits a sin worthy of excommunication (see 1 Cor. 5.11, 13b). God's children must keep themselves from uttering reviling words: speech of that nature must not be spoken.

Three

One who does the Lord's work must speak accurately. He should not be careless in his words. Only thus can he become a mouthpiece of the Lord and avoid many difficulties. We are deeply distressed by the fact that many times God's workman lacks restraint in speech, with the result that brothers and sisters relish his storytelling and his judgmental words but despise his preaching of God's word. Do not think that it does not matter if we speak wittily with our brothers and sisters today. Indeed, our speech may be very amusing. But wait until we stand up to preach the word of God, and then shall we see how they take it to be as amusing as was our storytelling. People will fail to respect what we say anymore.

One brother may speak and people listen, while another may speak and nobody listens. Why this difference? Do they not speak the same words? The word is of God all right, but one of them has spoken differently from the other in ordinary days on other matters. Let us recognize the fact that if two of us speak differently concerning other matters, and even though we both may speak forth the same word of God, the power of God's word will be different one from the other. For a person who speaks carelessly and without restraint in his daily speech will witness the same effect upon his hearers when he later preaches God's word. It will be as loose and powerless as before.

Let us not easily forget what we have learned from Scripture that a fountain does not send forth from the same opening both sweet water and bitter. It cannot yield up sweet fluid on one occasion and bitter fluid on another. Bitter water is always bitter. Though its bitterness may be somewhat diluted, it still remains bitter nonetheless. Note, too, that in mixing together clean and dirty water, the latter does not turn clean; instead, the former becomes dirty. Many brethren find that their power has been sapped not because they have done wrong in preaching God's word but because they have spoken wrongly in daily matters; so that no one will listen to them when they stand up to preach. Please be well advised that words uttered on the platform follow the words spoken off the platform. If you speak unwisely away from the podium, your speaking from the podium will be totally diluted, and the sweet water will have been turned bitter by you. We need not daily prepare the words which are to be delivered from the platform, but we ought to pay attention daily to the words used off the platform. How can we expect to manifest power in God's service if in our daily life we are undisciplined by speaking with carelessness, inaccuracy, distortion and jest, and even with outright lies? But having bridled our tongue in ordinary times from the outset, we may preach the word of the Lord.

Then, too, there is a close relationship between our speaking exactly and our studying of the Bible. For the

Bible is the most exact of books. There is but one set of words in the entire universe which is absolutely true, and that is what is found in the word of God. If we lack the habit of speaking accurately, we are not able to study the Bible nor to preach it. Judging by the way some brothers talk, we are forced to conclude that they have no possibility of studying God's word. Just as it demands a certain character in a person in order for him to *preach* God's word, so it requires a specific character in him who would *study* God's word. A careless person can never handle the Bible rightly. For the latter is most precise, and a careless person would only allow the word of God to leak away and thus misunderstand it.

Let us illustrate what exactness and precision here mean. Matthew 22 relates how the Sadducees did not believe in resurrection. They sought out the Lord Jesus and posed an apparently hard question to Him:

> Now there were with us seven brethren: and the first married and deceased, and having no seed left his wife unto his brother; and in like manner the second also, and the third, unto the seventh. And after them all, the woman died. In the resurrection therefore whose wife shall she be of the seven? for they all had her. (vv.25–28)

What they were suggesting was that resurrection was something unbelievable. It was best not to have resurrection, or else it would create great trouble and confusion. They came to reason with the Lord that if resurrection were true, the problem it created would be beyond solution.

But note how the Lord Jesus answered them:

Ye do err, not knowing the scriptures, nor the power of God. For in the resurrection they neither marry, nor are given in marriage, but are as angels in heaven. But as touching the resurrection of the dead, have ye not read that which was spoken unto you by God, saying, I am the God of Abraham, and the God of Isaac, and the God of Jacob? God is not the God of the dead, but of the living. (vv.29-32)

The Sadducees were those who had studiously pored over the Scriptures, yet the Lord said they did not understand them. And why? Because they were people who spoke carelessly; they never dreamed that God spoke so exactly.

Now in order to prove to His questioners the truth of resurrection, our Lord did not quote any other Scripture but the one in Exodus 3: "I am the God of Abraham, the God of Isaac, and the God of Jacob." Yet how in the world, the Sadducees must have thought, does this verse prove resurrection? "God is not the God of the dead, but of the living," said the Lord. Abraham had died, Isaac had died, and Jacob too had died. All three were dead and buried. Would we not therefore have to assume that God is the God of the dead since Jehovah God had himself declared that He is the God of Abraham, the God of Isaac, and the God of Jacob? Yet our Lord added that God is not the God of the dead but of the living! How can this apparent paradox be resolved? Well, since God is not the God of the dead, Abraham, though he is indeed a dead person today, shall one day become living. So shall Isaac and Jacob. But how *can* the dead become living? The answer: it must be through resurrection. Abraham will be resurrected, Isaac will be resurrected, and Jacob too will be resurrected simply because the God of Abraham, of Isaac, and of Jacob is not the God of the dead, but of the living. We see, then, how the Lord Jesus used these words to answer the question of the Sadducees. Note how very exact and precise was our Lord's speech. He showed them how they had erred due to their ignorance — yea, even their inaccurate handling — of the Scriptures as well as their ignorance of the power of God.

If we talk loosely, we will not be able to perceive the exactness of God's word. A careless disposition causes one to think inaccurately. He cannot be exact; therefore, he will allow to leak away the exact word of God. The Scriptures speak most truthfully. Every minute detail is exact. "One jot or one tittle," noted the Lord, "shall in no wise pass away from the law till all things be accomplished" (Matt. 5.18). The jots and tittles of each word which God uses are accentuated. They cannot be changed. And since God himself speaks with such exactitude, a servant of God must also speak in that manner.

Let us not fail to note that God's speaking is always solid. Every word of His is substantial and immovable. If you study the Bible and come to know it, you will confess that His word cannot have even one letter added to or taken away from it. We need to underline this point: that whoever speaks carelessly cannot be the Lord's servant. For he is not able to handle God's word rightly nor will he have any power or impact with brothers and sisters when he preaches. How distressful it is to listen to a given brother preaching whom you know very well. As you listen to him, you well know that he is an undisciplined person who speaks carelessly. With the result that when he stands up to preach he treats God's word lightly and loosely. Yet this should not surprise you, for how can he be careful on the platform when he has been so careless away from the platform? Let us realize that a careless undisciplined person can neither study the Bible well nor speak well for the Lord.

Let us ask God to show mercy towards us, causing us to speak accurately. We need to pray one prayer constantly, which is, to ask the Lord to give us the tongue of the instructed that we may not be a loose person who allows to be leaked away the testimony of God. A person who is unrestrained in speech can neither find out the facts of God's word well nor understand them. Let us therefore learn to speak carefully that we may also discover the exactness of each word in the Scriptures.

Four

Everyone who does the work of the Lord has his specialty. He has something particular in him which God can use. But he must also be normal in other areas so as to prevent any leakage. One may have something special in one area, but if he has a problem in another area, the power and effectiveness of his ministry will be drained away. The building blocks of character we have mentioned in the foregoing chapters — such as our being able to listen, to love mankind, have the mind to suffer, buffet the body, and be diligent and not slothful — are the most common qualities we must have. No servant of God can be lacking in these features. The restraint in speech which we are currently presenting is also one of the most common of qualities necessary to possess. For a person who speaks carelessly elsewhere can never utter God's word with accuracy at the time of preaching and teaching. Many brothers seemed to have a great future, but their power before God has totally leaked away due to their loose speech.

You must try your best to preserve the spiritual value, weight, and usefulness you possess before God. You cannot afford to let that which is special in you, or even what is ordinary, be gradually consumed. You must plug up every hole which leaks in order to preserve your ministry. The preservation of ministry is most essential to a workman of the Lord. Otherwise, whatever God has given to us or done in our lives will all be drained away from us. We should not be lax in a single one of these characteristics. And with respect to this current concern, we must allow the Holy Spirit to deal with all our speech and must accept whatever judgment necessary from God. It is not enough merely to possess this and the other positive features we have been discussing; in addition, we need to diligently preserve them continually so that nothing is diluted or leaks away. But especially is it true that any lack of restraint in speech will unquestionably drain away all these other positive features already obtained.

In our life ahead but prior to the judgment-seat of Christ, what destruction our speech causes to others will far surpass that from any other factor. This is because the destruction from speech does not stop with ourselves — it continues forth in touching other people. A word does not end when spoken. It reverberates throughout. A word once uttered cannot be called back even if you wanted to do so. You may repent, ask for forgiveness, and prostrate yourself in ashes, saying, "Lord, I have spoken inadvertently." But though the blood of Christ will most certainly cleanse you, it cannot eradicate that word from the world. That utterance will remain on earth. You may confess to the Lord and you may confess before your brother; moreover, the Lord may forgive you and so may your brother. But that word you spoke out of line will keep on spreading upon the earth. Some people may have a problem with the matter of cultivating a mind to suffer, or of the ability to listen, or of the lack of diligence; but no problem is more serious in its consequences than our being unrestrained in speech, since the death that is spread through our careless speaking or our much speaking or our inadvertent speaking will follow us to the very end.

For this reason, we are confronted with a most solemn issue here. Let us repent before God, because many words proceed from our mouth which are harmful instead of fruitful. Many words which come out of our mouth are idle words. And these idle words once uttered keep on spreading and are idle no longer. Though when we have spoken we have done so idly, our words after a while shall become rather busy and work busily. Hence let us plead for God's mercy that He will purify the past and deal with the present. May our lips be burnt as with coals (see Ps. 120.2-4 and also cf. Is. 6.5-7). For if our tongue be cleansed with burning coals, we shall not speak carelessly thereafter, thus diminishing the impact of many irretrievable situations. Many adverse situations once they occur are forever irretrievable. Lot, for example, could repent of his sin with his two daughters and be restored, but Moab and Ammon remain to the present day (see Gen. 19.30–38). Abraham gave birth to Isaac after his repentance with regard to Ishmael, but Isaac has forever had an adversary. Abraham might send Hagar away, yet the problem created has been prolonged indefinitely (see Gen. 21.8–14ff.). In similar fashion, a word once uttered never stops, and neither will the adverse effect it created ever pass away completely.

Therefore, we cannot but pray to the Lord: "O Lord, we need to have our tongue purified by fire so that we will no longer speak idle words, careless words, or outright lying words. Hereafter, cause us to have the tongue of the instructed" (see Is. 50.4). And once the Lord has been allowed to restrain our tongue from loose speaking, He will set us up as His mouth. Otherwise, it will always be inconceivable—yet quite true, nonetheless—that we can have two different waters—both sweet and bitter—coming forth from the same fountain. You declare that you wish to serve God and that you want to participate in His work. Yet how can you speak His word and speak the devil's word as well? You cannot. We must look to the Lord to be gracious to us that He put an end to our history of a "free" tongue and cause us to say to Him, "O Lord, let the words of my mouth be acceptable in Your sight even as the meditation of my heart is acceptable" (see Ps. 19.14). May the Lord have mercy upon us!

"For their sakes," prayed the Lord Jesus to His Father, "I sanctify myself" (John 17.19a). All who serve God, regardless the position they occupy, must learn to sanctify and set themselves apart. For the sake of serving people, we must sanctify ourselves in speech. How great a temptation speaking is! Whenever a few people are talking together, we are greatly tempted to join in with the talk. But let us learn to set ourselves apart by not falling in and talking loosely. Oh how our speech needs to be taught and our tongue to be instructed and disciplined (see Is. 50.4 mg., where the verse can also be rendered "the tongue of disciples" or "discipled ones"). Let our tongue be purified with burning coals and let us not fall into this temptation. Whenever some brothers and sisters are talking improperly, the first thing for us to do is to be sanctified from them, because the moment we join in with them, we shall fall. We must set ourselves apart from them as well as from their words. Each time such a situation occurs, do not yield to temptation but be separated. We trust God will have mercy upon us and gradually build in us His manifold grace.

7 | Be Stable

One

A workman of the Lord requires still another character feature. This we would call stability—a workman needs to be emotionally stable. Many before God are truly solid and firm, whereas many others are careless, unstable, and double-minded, and who oscillate according to their environment. This undependable nature does not stem from any lack of a desire to be trustworthy but from an unreliable character. Such individuals change with the weather. They are not solid. Yet God requires those who would serve Him to have a firm, reliable, and unshakable constitution.

In the Bible we can find one particularly easily shaken man. We all know that man to be Peter. But before examining in detail the weak, vacillating, and unreliable nature of Simon Peter's character, let us first consider a number of encouraging passages of Scripture that can give us all some hope in this area of concern now under discussion. First of all, we read:

Now when Jesus came into the parts of Caesarea
Philippi, he asked his disciples, saying, Who do men
say that the Son of man is? And they said, Some
say John the Baptist; some, Elijah; and others,
Jeremiah or one of the prophets. He saith unto
them, But who say ye that I am? And Simon Peter
answered and said, Thou art the Christ, the Son of
the living God. (Matt. 16.13-16)

Now on the basis of 1 John 5.1a ("Whosoever believeth
that Jesus is the Christ is begotten of God") and 5.13
("These things have I written unto you, that ye may
know that ye have eternal life, even unto you that believe
on the name of the Son of God"), we can assuredly
say that Peter would not have known those things he
uttered in his confession to Jesus at Caesarea Philippi
unless he had touched the life of God; for note the very
next verse: "Jesus answered and said unto him, Blessed art thou, Simon Bar-Jonah: for flesh and blood hath
not revealed it unto thee, but my Father who is in
heaven" (v.17). Please be aware of the fact that people
may be with Jesus, even sitting with Him and walking
with Him, but they will never know who Jesus is until
such inward knowledge as Peter received is revealed to
them by the Father who is in heaven.

Now let us pay close attention to verse 18a. Jesus
continued by saying: "And I also say unto thee, that
thou art Peter [Greek, *Petros*, stone], and upon this rock
[Greek, *petra*, rock] I will build my church." We ought
to realize that the true Church of God is not a shaking
entity. For the Church, as our Lord declared here, is
built on the rock. Let us keep this rock in mind as we
pursue our discussion further.

Here in Matthew 16 the Lord would seem to be touching indirectly on what He had spoken about on another occasion as recorded in Matthew 7. There He tells us that a person had built his house upon the sand; but then the rain descends, the floods come, and the wind blows, and that house is smitten; and it suddenly falls. But another person, Jesus went on to say, had built his house upon the rock; and though, as before, the rain descends, the floods come, and the wind blows, and these things beat upon that house, it does *not* fall (see vv.24–27). So that when the Lord subsequently declares that He will build His Church upon the rock, He shows us that His Church, like the house that is built upon the rock, will never fall. However much the rain may descend, the floods may arise, and the winds may blow, the House of God will not fall. Rains descending or not, floods coming or not, winds blowing or not — none of these constitutes any problem to this spiritual House. For it is built upon rock; and consequently, the Church is stable, fall-proof, and unshakable. Such is the basic nature of the Church.

Note, too, that when Paul wrote to Timothy, he called "the house of God . . . the church of the living God, the pillar and ground of the truth" (1 Tim. 3.15). The Church is like a pillar which is fixed firmly and cannot be shaken. It does not matter much if one shakes a chair, but to shake a house is of great concern. The fundamental nature of the Church is that it is built upon the Rock which is stable and unshakable. All the children of God who are built upon this Rock are stones. Peter himself wrote in this very same vein much later in his first letter: "ye also, as living stones, are built up a spiritual house" (2.5a). Each and every brother and sister is a living stone being built upon the Rock. So that in this construction, whatever is underneath is that which is above. Whatever the foundation is it is the same kind of material that the superstructure is, and vice-versa.

In the Church there are no bricks, only stones. By sharp contrast, the tower of Babel had been built with bricks, for it had been constructed by men working with imitation stones. But in the Church there are no bricks, nothing of man-made imitations. The Church is built upon the Rock. Each one of us is like a stone before the Lord. And these stones are built together to be a spiritual House. So that we can very clearly see that the Church of God has this basic nature of stability.

Now following upon all this, the Lord then makes this declaration: "and the gates of Hades shall not prevail against it" (Matt. 16.18b). As we have seen, this unshakable thing of which the Lord speaks is called the Church. Its foundation is Rock which is something unshakable and firm, and its building or superstructure is of like material—that is, of stones—which is likewise not to be shaken. But if all this be true, then how can the ministries in the Church be found so often to be shakable and unreliable? This is the very matter we intend to talk about in our discussion from this point forward. Do please be very clear here that we are not discussing the matter of the *Church*; rather, we are going to deal with this matter of the *ministers in* the Church. When the Lord told Simon, "Thou art Peter," He meant, "You are a stone." Peter here represents all the ministers in the Church. All who work and serve must be stones. Though these stones are not as massive as the Rock, they nonetheless bear the same nature as the Rock which is that of firmness and unshakableness. Here, therefore, we see that a minister must also not be shaken, for is he not a stone? Yet we all know only too well that unfortunately too many *are* shaken and unreliable. And this is the very problem we hope now to address.

Proceeding further, we note that the Lord continued in His teaching by saying: "I will give unto thee the keys of the kingdom of heaven: and whatsoever thou shalt bind on earth shall be bound in heaven; and whatsoever thou shalt loose on earth shall be loosed in heaven" (Matt. 16.19). The promise the Lord gives to the Church is also given to Peter. For please note that while in Matthew 18.18 (and cf. v.17) we see this promise given to the Church, here in Matthew 16 it is given to Peter personally. All this indicates that our Lord views Peter as a minister of the Church. The Lord gives him the keys of the kingdom of heaven that he may open its door. And we believe that following the Lord's resurrection and ascension Peter did indeed open the door of the kingdom of heaven — first on the the Day of Pentecost and later in the house of Cornelius. He opened the door to both the Jews and the Gentiles.

Now as Peter — that is, as a stone — he can use the keys. But whenever he is *not* a Peter, that is to say, not a *stone*, he cannot use the keys. Today, not all who are called Peter are really Peter, just as not all who are called Israel are strong. A person's name may indeed be Israel, but he is still a weak person. Here is a man whose name is Peter; to him the Lord gives the keys. When he is really

Peter, when he is truly a stone, he can use the keys. Whatsoever he binds shall be bound, and whatsoever he looses shall be loosed.

Hence, the acceptable inward constitution of a minister is found in his stable character. This is a fundamental requirement. When a person is wavering, he cannot be a minister before God, nor can the Church follow him. Some brothers and sisters have this underlying defect in character. They are easily shaken, always changing, ever oscillating. They are not stable and solid before God. Such people cannot serve the Church because they are not able to stand firm, and consequently they will be prevailed upon by the gates of Hades.

Thank God for using Peter as an example in His word. God looks for such a man whose nature is the same as that of the foundation of the Church. The one who ministers must be a solid stone. Thank the Lord for choosing Peter as a sample, thus assuring *us* who later follow that He is able to transform *us* into such stability even as He eventually did in Simon Peter. This man here is indeed called Peter, yet he does not look like a Peter. His name is truly "a stone," but his personality is like flowing water that constantly shifts its course: sometimes he is resolute, at other times he is vacillating; sometimes he is strong, at other times he is weak. The Lord puts him before us in order to teach us that before anyone is dealt with by God, his temperament is rather irresolute. Before he becomes a stone he cannot use the keys, neither is he of any special use before God. Not until his weak disposition is dealt with by the Lord can he be used by God.

We thank the Lord that human character may be

changed. It is not something unchangeable. Like Peter, a vacillating person can be transformed into a stable person. Under the burning light of the Lord, your tongue can be so purified that though you were by nature talkative you now become a man of few words. Under the reproach of the Lord, the laziness of the slothful dies out. When the Lord cursed the fig tree, it withered from the root. For where the Lord's reproach and curse is, there is withering and death. If you have not met the Lord deeply, you may be able to live on in a happy-go-lucky manner. But once you have truly met Him, your flippant nature is shrivelled up. By the touch of the Lord's light, whether it comes by listening to the preaching of God's word or through the open reproach of a brother, you are undone. At the reproach of the Lord, you come to your end.

What we are therefore saying here concerns the formation of character or, more accurately said, the reconstruction in character. Many have a weak disposition, one which is inattentive, cold or lazy, but when they are met by the Lord, they shrink under God's enlightenment. How gracious the Lord is in selecting Peter; else all the weak and wavering among us will consider themselves to be hopeless. Our Lord chooses a man, names him Peter, transforms him to be a stone, then puts the keys of the kingdom of heaven into his hand and brings him to the Church.

Two

The Scriptures tell us that Peter confessed the Lord to be the Christ, the Son of the living God. And the

Lord's immediate comment and response was: "flesh and blood hath not revealed it unto thee, but my Father who is in heaven." All this is God's doing. On Peter's side, there is not the slightest work. He received here the revelation of the Father, which revelation could not be known by flesh and blood, not even by *his* flesh and blood. Following this we read a most ominous and startling passage: "From that time began Jesus to show unto his disciples, that he must go unto Jerusalem, and suffer many things of the elders and chief priests and scribes, and be killed, and the third day be raised up. And Peter took him, and began to rebuke him, saying, Be it far from thee, Lord: this shall never be unto thee. But he turned, and said unto Peter, Get thee behind me, Satan" (Matt. 16.21–23a). What we would call attention to is the contrast between the revelation Peter received as recorded in the foregoing passage and his now being used by Satan as revealed in this present passage. We may say that in the former instance Peter met the heavenly Father, but here in this instance he met Satan. Earlier he could confess to Jesus: "Thou art the Christ, the Son of the living God"; now, though, he could tell Him: "Be it far from thee, Lord: this shall never be unto thee." The moral and spiritual distance between these two is as the physical distance between the North Pole and the South!

If we understand rightly, the revelation Peter received is the highest ever recorded in the four Gospels. It is the Father who gave Peter this revelation of knowing Jesus as the Christ, the Son of the living God. It is the Lord himself who showed Peter that the Church is to be built on the Rock of this understanding. In fact, the revelation Peter obtained here is so vast in significance that it was not even seen by those others who were closest to the Lord Jesus nor by His other followers. Most probably, it can be stated with a good deal of confidence that what Peter saw is the peak revelation anyone can receive. Yet equally great was Simon Peter's fall, for he soon fell to the lowest valley. He spoke not only out of his flesh; he actually spoke as well according to Satan. Formerly, he had spoken according to the Father, but now he changed into speaking according to Satan. This was unquestionably a one-hundred-and-eighty-degree shift! Were the Church to be built on such a minister as this, it would certainly be prevailed against by the gates of Hades. The Church cannot be built by such a vacillating person because it requires stone-like people to build it.

The ministers of the Church must be stable like stones. They should not speak according to God and then turn about and do so according to God's Enemy. This is a serious matter. Peter fell to the lowest point only a short while after he had received the highest revelation. He tried to block the Lord from going to the cross. He did not continue to mind the things of God, and thus he was used by God's Archenemy. When Satan's word was uttered by Simon Peter, the gates of Hades were at that moment opened. If Satan and the gates of Hades were to gain the victory, the Church would be defeated. Unless the Lord were to transform Simon Peter into a solid stone, the Church would have little hope.

Today we need stable ministers, those as dependable and unshakable as stones. We must not think and talk of one thing now and think and talk of another thing next. If we are truly solid and firm before God, there will be blessings in the Church, and the gates of Hades shall not prevail against it. If we are weak and wavering, Satan will be able to speak and the gates of Hades shall instantly be opened. The case before us with Peter serves as an extreme contrast. The distance it spans is very far. Nevertheless, it does cause us to know what kind of person Peter naturally was.

On another occasion, the Lord Jesus, upon concluding His last supper with His disciples, said to them: "All ye shall be offended in me this night: for it is written, I will smite the shepherd, and the sheep of the flock shall be scattered abroad." But Peter answered and said to Him, "If all shall be offended in thee, I will never be offended" (Matt. 26.31,33). According to his temperament, what Peter said was true. He was not lying, and he would not lie. Let us recall, however, that at the time of our own consecration or personal revival, many words we uttered before the Lord were beyond our comprehension. The same must have been true with especially the kind of emotional person Peter was, for not surprisingly he would indeed be likely to say, "I will never be offended." Though he was like this emotionally, he was not like this as a person.

Many people who are full of emotion need, for the purpose of better understanding and dealing with themselves, to learn how to separate their emotion from their own selves. Sooner or later, they shall come to realize that their emotion does not actually represent them. Some people may live predominantly by their thought life. They are the kind who depend on their brain. When they pray, they pray with their mind. They do not know the difference between the mind and the heart. They follow their mind to such a degree that their heart is never released. They in fact consider their mind as their heart. One day, however, they receive light and suddenly become aware that their mind is not their heart.

There are many others—like Simon Peter—who sense their heart becoming strangely warm. They feel they really love the Lord. They can quite easily say, "I love the Lord," and truly mean it emotionally. Yet if they were to be challenged to the effect that their feeling is not fact, their reply would be, "If *I* do not love the Lord, then who does?" But just wait until the day when their feelings are dealt with, and then they shall see that their heart and their emotion are two different things. Their feeling is not really themselves. They and their emotion are vastly separated even as their mind is separated from their own selves.

Now Peter was here speaking according to his emotion. He thought his feeling spoke for him. As he was declaring, "I will never be offended," he did not recognize that the "I" was not he himself but was his emotion. He did not realize how tightly his outward man was wrapped around him nor how deeply he lived in the outward man. He did not know his own word, not even his own self. The Lord responded to Peter by saying: "Verily I say unto thee, that this night, before the cock crow, thou shalt deny me thrice" (v.34). Yet even these dramatic words did not bring Peter up short, for Peter still did not know himself, with the result that he next boldly asserted and declared to the Lord, "Even if I must die with thee, yet will I not deny thee" (v.35a).

The facts before us betray two extremes. On the one side, Peter told the Lord he would never be offended in Him; on the other side, he denied Jesus three times. On the one hand, he declared he would die with the Lord; on the other hand, not only did he not die with the Lord, he even trembled at the accusation of a harmless maid servant that he had been with Jesus. These two extremes show us how easily swayed this man was. Though his name was Peter, his temperament was nonetheless like flowing water, changing according to circumstances. He was completely governed by his surroundings. In the Garden of Gethsemane, for example, he fell asleep as did the other disciples. He had loudly proclaimed, "If all shall be offended in thee, I will never be offended," yet he proceeded to go to sleep just as the others did in the Garden.

So the temperament of this person is quite plainly revealed: at one moment he spoke with such confidence and feeling, but at the next moment he is seen as acting in a very opposite manner. He lived in his feeling instead of living in his real person. An individual can live so long in his emotion that he fails to know himself, because he has come to think his feeling is himself. And such was this man whom we have come to know as Peter. He said he would never be offended, and he really thought so. Yet even before he had had any confrontation, he had already fallen asleep in the Garden of Gethsemane. His spirit was willing, but his flesh was weak.

A little later, Peter stirred up himself, drew out a

sword and cut off an ear of the high priest's servant (see Matt. 26.51 with John 18.10). Peter loved the Lord so much that he dared to do such a thing for His sake. He totally disregarded his own personal safety. Doubtless he had at this point climbed fairly high in his own estimation of himself. A moment later, however, and he again fell to a great depth. Such a man was Peter.

Concerning Peter's denial of the Lord, Mark 14 tells us that at first "Peter had followed" Jesus "afar off, even within, into the court of the high priest; and he was sitting with the officers, and warming himself in the light of the fire" (v.54). When a maid of the high priest caught sight of him and then said, "Thou also wast with the Nazarene, even Jesus" (v.67 with v.66), Peter denied it, saying, "I neither know, nor understand what thou sayest" (v.68). How could a man who had followed the Lord for three and a half years have no knowledge of who the Lord was? In one moment he was bravely slashing with the sword, but in another moment his courage wilted and completely failed him. While the Lord's own courage stood firm as He was being judged harshly and humiliated by all, Peter's courage deserted him under the mildest of circumstances. A moment ago, he had truly been willing to die for the Lord; now he really loved his own life too much. He had shifted from one extremity to the other.

A second time the maid spoke, yet not to Peter but to those who stood by. She said to them in Peter's hearing: "This is one of them." The first time the maid had directly addressed Peter: "Thou also wast with the Nazarene, even Jesus"—and the Lord's disciple had denied such a connection. Now, though, Peter was in the porch (or forecourt area) when this same maid, see-ing him again, spoke about him to those who stood by, she merely saying, "This is one of them." Yet Peter once again denied his connection with the Lord and His followers (vv.69–70). According to the record of Mat-thew, Peter in his denial this second time "denied with an oath, I know not the man" (26.72).

And after a little while, those who stood by said to Peter, "Of a truth thou art one of them; for thou art a Galilean." But Peter began "to curse, and to swear," he this time emphatically declaring: "I know not this man of whom ye speak" (Mark 14.70–71). Yes, indeed, Peter cursed and swore! Earlier he had denied with an oath; now he denied with cursing and swearing.

Can we see the picture here? When the maid first spoke to him, he denied the accusation and left for the porch, most likely because he thought the place where he and the maid had been was too dangerous. But when he heard the maid speak again to those who stood by the porch to the effect that he was one of the Nazarene company, he again denied—this time with an oath— that he did not know the Man. Later, when those who stood by challenged him as being one of the Nazarene company, he denied with cursing and swearing.

Three different words are employed in connection with Peter's denial. At the second instance, it was with an "oath" (Greek, *horkos*). At the third instance, it was accompanied by his beginning "to curse" (Greek, *anathematizō*) and "to swear" (Greek, *omnumi*). He used all kinds of expletives, both oath and curse and swearword. At the second denial, he did so by invok-ing the name of God and swearing by heaven and earth.

On the third occasion he even cursed with swearing. He not only drew upon God to prove that he did not know the Man but he also called down a curse upon himself if he knew the Man. How greatly he had fallen!

Here was a man who could not represent a true Peter, that is to say, a Peter stable as a stone. For he vacillated all the time. He rose so high as to touch heaven; then he fell so low as to be used by Satan. At his height he could declare that even if all others were offended in Jesus he would never be offended; at his low point he would fall asleep. He was so bold as to draw a sword and cut off the right ear of Malchus; but then he became so frightened even before a maid that he denied the Lord with an oath and a curse. Without question, such a person possessed a great defect in his character.

Three

Why would a man such as this be so unsettled? Ordinarily speaking, there are three basic reasons: The first is because this person is emotional; the second is because he is afraid of loss, pain, and the cross, and hence he desires to please himself; and third is because he is fearful of men and their displeasure, inasmuch as he wants to please them and enjoy a peaceful happy environment. These are the basic reasons for instability of character.

Peter was precisely this kind of person. He was governed by emotion. One who lives according to feeling is easily changeable. He may touch Heaven at one moment and be used by Heaven's Enemy the next.

Human emotion is highly undependable. We have yet to see a person who can sustain his emotion for long. For if he lives by feeling, he lives by the stimuli supplied by emotion. And thus he is frequently found swaying from cold to hot and hot to cold. This person may on the one hand receive Heaven's revelation through the mercy of God and on the other hand say as moved by his own feeling, "Be it far from thee, Lord: this shall never be unto thee." Peter attempted to block the Lord in the latter's intended path as though he knew better than the Lord. That is why he took hold of Jesus and rebuked Him. All who are emotional tend to offer advice and act impulsively as counsellors. They seem to know what to do in every situation. They are prone to act on a moment's impulse. They feel quickly and act quickly.

In the light of all this that has been said, we ought to learn to be dealt with in this basic character flaw. We who are easily stirred should not deceive ourselves that we are far different from Peter. No, no—the truth is, is it not, that we are fairly close to him. Such weakness in character poses a great problem in our work for the Lord. Unless this problem is solved, Pentecost will not come. We must not live according to our feeling. We must not live by emotional stimuli. We should control our feeling, for such improper impulses cause us to sway from left to right, right to left, up and down, and down and up. This is not of the Lord but is from our corrupted natural man. If we permit this element to govern us, we will be of little use in the work of God.

Only the weakest of men follow their emotion. Such a way of life signifies weakness, not strength. The strong are able to control themselves. They have their eyes well opened not to trust in their own emotion. Only those who do not trust their feeling, but instead subject it to their control, will learn how not to live by feeling. Otherwise, they will incorrectly assume that their feeling is their own selves.

Peter was a forthright person. He uttered what he saw and felt. And he honestly thought that what he said was true. In the eyes of other men, he was upright and honest, impulsive and undiplomatic. Yet a person such as this, who lives so much by his emotion, is useless in spiritual work. He must be dealt with.

Now I know that many of you *feel* you love the Lord, but let me say that you possibly have not truly loved the Lord. You may wish to live for the Lord, yet possibly you have not really lived for Him. For you yourself are more than your feeling and much deeper than your emotion. You may think you are willing to die for the Lord, yet you do not truly know yourself. You fail to discern who the "I" is who professes to love, to live for and to be willing to die on behalf of the Lord. That which is outside of feeling and yet deeper than feeling is your real "I." Peter mistook his outward man to be his real person. He did not know that the one who declared a willingness to die for the Lord was his emotional, outward man. Sometime later, however, his actual condition became self-evident to him. From this we can conclude that a person whose emotion has not been broken by the Lord will always live by his feeling. He changes ever so often. He may consider himself to be wholly true; nevertheless, he is actually governed by his emotion.

We know it is a despicable thing to lie. How pitiful if we do not know we are lying. By the same token, the undependableness of our emotion is most lamentable, and our not knowing its undependability is likewise deplorable. It is foolish for anyone to take for granted that he is what he feels. One day he may need to fail as terribly as Peter did in order to realize that his feeling and his own self are different the one from the other. Peter felt one way at the last supper with our Lord, but he felt differently in the Garden of Gethsemane. The feeling he had at his exit from the Garden (when he slashed the servant's ear off) was quite different from that which he had in the porch. Blessed is the man who is able to differentiate between himself and his feeling. Only the fool reckons his feeling as his own self. All who have been truly taught by God will understand that feeling is not themselves.

Do we all see this? Our emotional impulse is not our self. Judging by impulse, you might deem Peter to be a heavenly man who would never fall; for on behalf of the Lord did he not draw his sword and cut off the right ear of Malchus? But judging spiritually, Peter's emotion was not Peter himself. His feeling was courageous, yet his person was cowardly. He felt he loved the Lord, though he loved his own life more. He wished to lay down his life; nevertheless, he wanted to protect himself. If the Church is led by such a minister as this, the Church will shake and quake with her minister, and the gates of Hades shall certainly prevail. It becomes clear that God cannot use this kind of person to lead and build His Church.

We noted earlier that Peter was fearful of loss. A

chief reason for instability is this fear of loss. Many are brave before they meet the cross and encounter trials and distresses. But when the time comes for them to forsake all things, even their very lives, they shrink back from such a cross. In ordinary days, all seem to love the Lord and are willing to bear the cross, but at a critical moment they are unable to persevere. Why is this? Because of the fear of loss and the love of self.

Here lies the problem with Peter. What happened in the porch merely put into stark relief the fact of what kind of person he himself was when he confronted the Lord at Caesarea Philippi. His fear of loss and love of self did not begin in the porch, for when he stood up to the prophecy of the Lord's impending Calvary experience, he quickly blurted out: "Be it far from thee, Lord: this shall never be unto thee." Because he himself was this kind of person — namely, desirous of avoiding any cross or loss or pain for himself — he therefore offered such advice to the Lord. Peter himself was afraid of loss and of death. In reality he hoped for *himself* that "this shall never be." He rebelled to such a degree as to lay hold of the Lord physically and rebuke Him. Only one kind of person is stable, and that is those who are faithful before God even unto death. Satan can do nothing to such people. The weakest are those who love their own lives. For as soon as they are confronted with issues of life and death, they immediately fall. Simon Peter was such a man. His advice to the Lord was nothing short of this: "Lord, never go to the cross." Later on, while the Lord Jesus was on trial, Peter used various means to keep himself from the cross. He even uttered oaths and cursed and swore.

To have the mind to suffer is therefore a major problem. Having subsequently learned before the Lord, Peter later spoke well on this subject. He knew his failure and had learned his lesson. He now *armed* himself with the mind to suffer (see 1 Peter 4.1), a weapon of spiritual warfare he had not possessed before. No one who is fearful is strong. We must learn to be brought to the place where we can say to the Lord: "O Lord, I will gladly bear Your cross and willingly bear all losses. I will not seek my own profit or pleasure." Satan can do nothing to a person who stands on this ground. You will become a strong person if you are not afraid of loss and pain, if, like Job, you can say, "Though he [God] slay me, yet will I trust in him" (Job 13.15 AV), or if, like Madame Guyon, you can declare as she did that she would kneel and kiss the whip which God used to deal with her. He who cannot be shaken by the cross cannot be shaken by anything, for there is nothing in the world that demands more than the cross of Jesus. If you are able to answer the greatest demand, you will doubtless be able to answer all other smaller demands. On the other hand, if you are not able to take up the cross and follow the Lord, you will unquestionably fall at the touch of any adversity. You shall not be stable but shall easily be shattered.

Hence we must believe in the fact of the cross and enter into its experience. Whatever trial, distress, or pain given by God must be accepted with submission. You will then consider any affliction the world may press upon you to be light. The reason you today have difficulty is because you do not know the cross. You have not met the largest test (the cross), and so you fall at the smallest test. Had you passed the largest trial you would not have been shaken by the smallest trial. Peter was shattered because he was fearful of loss and pain and because of his self-love.

Yet there remains another reason for Peter's fluctuation—which is, that he lived according to circumstances. He looked for smooth sailing and was afraid of people's opinion. Alas, the pressure of human affection is far greater than we can imagine, and the fear of people's displeasure is deeper than we like to think possible. The moment we try to please men or to avoid their displeasure, we shall walk a crooked path. We will direct our speech to suit the people before us and will listen far too much to what people say—even as did Peter, who was afraid of the maid and afraid of those others who stood by at the porch. At such a moment we, like him, shall be truly bound by weakness.

Do you want to please men or do you wish to please God? You ought to have this question settled the first day you offer yourself to serve Him. If you still insist on pleasing men, you cannot and will not suffer the offense of the cross. How can you walk the straight path if you have not settled this issue of the fear of men? Such fear will constantly affect your walk before God. You will never be stable and strong.

Four

The nature of the Church, as we have seen, is stone-like; but so, too, must the nature of its ministers be. The foundation of the Church is Rock, and its superstructure is stones. And hence its service must be all of stones as well, with neither any variation nor shadow of turning (cf. James 1.17b). Whatever is weak, vacillating or shaky cannot make any valuable contribution in the ongoing work of God. Only what is strong, stable, and firm is trustworthy. As one stone is placed upon another, the whole structure shall collapse if any one of the stones becomes undependable.

Let it be clearly understood that in the Church of God, you are not the last stone—there are numerous other stones to be added onto you. The Church is not tens of thousands of stones lying scattered about. It is built with stones upon stones upon stones until she becomes a spiritual House. Whenever a stone is not upon another stone, the Church will be in ruin. The tearing down and ultimate destruction of the temple in Jerusalem was predicted by our Lord to His disciples in terms of there not being one stone left upon another (see Matt. 24.1–2). But note that the building up of the Holy Temple of God (as represented by the Christians) is described by Peter in terms of living stones being built up as a spiritual house (see 1 Peter 2.5). Today God is building many people and incorporating many things. One stone is added onto another. In the event one stone is shaken, it will create a tremendous disaster, for many will be hurt and the Church will not be able to move forward.

For this reason, our character needs to become stone-like, wholly reliable. Otherwise, the whole structure will be adversely affected by our shaky temperament, and it will eventually crash. Let us instead heed Paul's admonition: "be ye steadfast, unmovable, always abounding in the work of the Lord" (1 Cor. 15.58). The pathway of service lies in unmovable perseverance. A weak character that vacillates will spoil the work of God.

Why are many brothers and sisters unable to do the Lord's work? It is due to their undependableness. In the face of such lack of dependability, whatever is built will be totally torn down, and furthermore, there will be a waste of time. What is destroyed may be equal to what is built, but the time wasted cannot be restored. In the case of the reliable, whatever is built stays and no time is lost. But if there be destruction, and though reconstruction may begin anew, the loss of ten or twenty years would nonetheless be irreparable. Hence let us ask God to make us reliable. We may not climb as high as did Peter, for that requires time; but we may at least be stable and dependable so that we will not see torn down what has been built up.

If we are stable and dependable, we will dutifully perform the responsibility laid upon us. Otherwise, when we are called to keep watch, we will fall asleep. An unreliable person is suddenly high and suddenly low. He cannot watch and pray, because he must sleep. Since he needs eight hours of sleep, he does not recognize the importance of watching. Do you realize how great is such a loss? When the Lord calls you to watch, will you go to sleep instead? If so, then when later He calls you to work, how can you possibly respond? You will not have a sense of responsibility.

A man who is unstable is unreliable, and an unreliable person has no sense of responsibility. When he feels elated, he can do much; but when he feels low, he will go to sleep, thus evincing a lack of responsibility. A stable character is therefore a fundamental requirement. Only a person with a character like that may do the work of God. He will work whether he feels comfortable, elated, or depressed. He will work come rain or come shine. He is a stable person. But an unstable character is affected by many things, even by the weather. How can a work of the Lord be done by such a person as this? We need to have a strong spirit before God.

Let me ask: are you a reliable person? a stable person? an immovable person? You will find that the keys shall be given to you only when one day you have learned the lesson God wants you to learn. These keys are to open the doors of the gospel to the Jews and the Gentiles. And the Church will be built. In order to build up the House of God, the Lord shall look everywhere for reliable, stable ministers before He can begin to build His House. Once God has His useful ministers, then the doors in many localities will be opened. But if these ministers — these servants of God — are unreliable, weak and vacillating, such doors will never be opened.

Thank God, Peter saw his weakness through failure. He fell terribly. He wept much and bitterly, for he at last knew his corruption. Many brothers and sisters, like Peter was, are equally weak and shaky. May we, even as Peter must have done, tell God, "Lord, I am undone!" Have we not asked for enlightenment? Let us understand that oftentimes terrible failure is itself an enlightenment, just as is strong reproof or convicting preaching. Man ought to fall before the word of God. He should submit to strong reproof. Likewise, man needs to prostrate himself in the face of terrible failure. For such failure can bring light: God can show man what he really is.

We know that when Peter fell, he went out into the night and wept bitterly (see Matt. 26.75b and Luke 22.62). Under the merciful hand of God, he became a true Peter. From a weak and shaky individual he was transformed into a stable and solid man. He was used to open the door of the gospel to the Jews on the Day of Pentecost and to Gentiles later in the house of Cornelius (Acts chapters 2 and 10). May God be gracious to us that there will be a transformation in our character too. Our character needs to be changed, and only the Lord is able to transform it: the lazy will become diligent; the talkative will grow quiet; those unable to listen will now listen; those fearful of suffering will have the mind to suffer; and the uncontrolled will be disciplined. But so also, the weak, shaky, and vacillating will become strong, steadfast, and immovable.

8 | Must Not Be Subjective

One

Subjectivity is another major problem among God's children. Especially when identified with the Lord's workmen, subjectivity can spoil God's work.

What is subjectivity? It is an insistence upon one's own opinion while refusing to accept the opinion of others. Before one even hears people, his mind is already made up, so that after he has heard what another has said, he still insists on his own idea. This is called subjectivity. A subjective person finds it hard to accept the thoughts of others and is not easily corrected. He forms his idea from the outset and insists on it to the very end. Before the Lord has spoken, before any fact has been revealed, or before people have expressed their opinions, the subjective person has already come up with his own preconceived idea. Even after the Lord has spoken, the fact has been revealed or other people's opinions have been expressed, his preconceived notion remains unmoved. This is called subjectivity. The basic cause for this condition is man's unbroken self; consequently, he maintains a stiff prejudice which is not easily forsaken or corrected.

Two

What are the problems caused by subjectivity? What are the damages a subjective person brings about? A brother or sister who is this way is not able to listen. To counteract this subjective tendency we must learn to listen to both God and man. The word of man as well as the word of God can only enter in where the mind is open. For the subjective person, an open mind becomes a real problem. So that a basic requirement for accomplishing the Lord's work is to be able to listen so as to know the situation of others. We have mentioned before that an inability to listen creates a major difficulty for a workman of the Lord. The principal reason for such inability is subjectivity. Due to such a state one's inside is piled full with unbreakable and unchangeable thoughts. A person's own words and affairs fully occupy him. So that when a brother or a sister comes to that person and lays his or her burden before him, the latter may hear and yet not hear at all. This is the predicament that a subjective person always finds himself in — and is one of his own making.

Three

A subjective person has another problem: he finds it difficult to learn anything. How can he learn any further when he is already so confident, so clear, so sure, so decided on everything in his mind? He has his set ideas on all matters. In the case of some young workers, for them to be able to learn would be almost like forcing medicine down the throat of a child. They are so full of opinions, ideas and ways that they seem to know everything. Though they may not profess to be omnipotent, they do appear to be omniscient. To teach them anything is a more difficult task than it would be to coerce them to take medicine. If a person must be spoon-fed, how much food can he consume in his lifetime? Is it not true that when you meet such a brother, are you not tempted to say, "Brother, I wonder how much you will be able to learn in your lifetime?" The greatest deficiency in a subjective person is his inability to learn. Each time you wish to help him do so, you have to fight as it were with him. If the Lord's workman can shed his subjectivity, he shall be able to receive help quickly.

Now we know that the helps we receive come from all sides, and we also know that there are many things we need to learn. Yet how much are we taking in if we learn only one thing in one month, in half a year, or even a whole year? Furthermore, a subjective person tends to become even more subjective and increasingly less able to learn as the years go by. What a great blight upon the Church subjectivity truly is!

Although the path a workman of the Lord travels needs to be straight and stable, his ideas and views should not be so fixed and immovable that he has little chance to learn and is of very little use in his lifetime. We must be stable in character on the one hand and yet not subjective in mind on the other. God's children need to learn not to be this way so that they may be easily moved by the Lord. The way to judge if one is subjective or not is to note whether he learns, and if so, how fast he does so. Is he able to learn spiritual things many times and all the time? That which obstructs the ability to learn is subjectivity.

To make progress in spiritual things we must be open to God—both our spirit, our heart, and our mind. To be open means not to be subjective. It is true that having the spirit open to God is something deeper than not being subjective. Nevertheless, the first and essential step is our not being subjective. As long as we are the latter, the door to revelation is locked. Not being subjective indicates that we are tender and teachable and able to be impressed. Many, however, are hard to be impressed by God. For them to receive any impression God must employ a whip, a rod, or even a hammer to beat upon them. We need to learn the lesson that by the mere moving of God's eyes we instantly understand. Yet many people are like horses: unless there be bit and bridle or even a whip, there will be no understanding. This is called subjectivity.

God may strive with a subjective person, bring him to his end, and allow him to be badly beaten, yet he is struggling all the time and is not able to yield quickly to learn the necessary lesson. Oh, how many of God's children are not soft and gentle before Him. Instead, they are hard and stubborn. Such ones have great difficulty in God's work, for they learn little and therefore contribute little. This is a great loss.

Four

A subjective person has another problem: he is unable to obtain the Lord's guidance. He cannot touch God's will, nor can he follow His leading. Those who are subjective cannot know the divine will because to receive guidance one needs to be tender and teachable— traits which are lacking in the subjective person. But as soon as the one who is teachable hears God speaking, he immediately obeys. He is no longer subjective.

Balaam's heart inclined itself towards wealth, and so he conceived a preferred view. He was determined to go to the place of his own appointment, not God's; therefore, he prayed once and again until God let him go. It is not easy for one whose mind is already made up to know the Lord's will. We must learn to walk in the will of the Lord. We know that along the path of His will we sometimes are required to stop immediately and sometimes to commence right away. What would you do if you were ready to move and the Lord wanted you to stop? If the Spirit of the Lord does not allow you to go, can you stop? A subjective person cannot. But he who has learned to listen to God is not subjective. He has learned to hearken to His word so that he is able to go or to stop at God's command.

Do not view these words as too elementary. Please be advised that a subjective person finds it hard to begin moving at God's order, and even if he has begun to move, he may not halt at God's word. Here is the problem. It takes much energy to move a subjective person, and once he does move, he cannot be stopped. Not so, however, with the man who has learned. He is so flexible in the Lord's hand that he can easily be moved or stopped at His command. Such a person receives the guidance of God. Others must be heavily whipped by the Lord before they will move, and then, no one thereafter can *stop* them. They will need another heavy-handed dealing of God to make them stop. Their subjectivity makes it difficult for them to know and to do the divine will.

The offering up of Isaac by Abraham provides an excellent illustration of not being subjective. God called Abraham to offer up his son. If such a demand were to come upon a subjective person, it would not be easily done, if at all; for such a one would have had many things to say: he would have argued that he had had no say and had not thought of having a son, that he had been quite satisfied with having his chief servant Eliezer of Damascus—"one born in my house" (see Gen. 15.2–3), but that God had given him the son Isaac: neither he nor Sarah had had any idea—it was the Lord who had done this: how, then, could God who had done all this now ask him to offer up Isaac as a burnt-offering? Let us see that a subjective person would have had plenty of reasons indeed to reject such a demand.

Abraham, on the other hand, was simple like a child. He found no difficulty with the Lord's command. He believed that God was able to raise his son from the dead. As he was ready to lift up the knife and kill Isaac on the altar, God provided a ram as a substitute (see Gen. 22.10,13). Had Abraham been a subjective man, all this that God had done and was now asking would have created a problem for him. A subjective Abraham would have been perplexed by seemingly contradictory words from God. But not so with the Abraham of the Bible. He was not at all subjective. Some may find it hard to be placed on the altar; but equally so, once there, they find it hard to come down from the altar. It might take a number of years for him to get there; but then, living or dead, he may refuse to come down. In the area of obedience, a subjective person follows his own idea. He cannot stop even when God wants him to stop. He will not obey till he is pressed to the wall, and his obedience is according to his own strength. Once a step is taken, he is beyond retrieving even at the command of God.

How do you tame a wild horse so that someone can ride on it? It is quite difficult to train such an animal. In order to tame it, you need a good horseman who is able to jump on its back and ride on it. You then allow the horse to run and strive until it is totally exhausted. Then you can control it. The good horseman has the skill to keep himself on the horse's back and not fall off. He will let the animal run until it finally realizes that there is nothing it can do but obey. Such a horseman is able to train a wild horse to such a degree that it finally will perform a perfect circle act. The training required is as follows. A pole is planted in the center of a small circle, and a rope is attached from the pole to the horse. If the latter runs a slightly wider circle, the rope will break; and if it runs a little closer, the rope is no longer taut. A trained horse can trot hundreds of times around the pole and the radius will remain the same all the time. And when this ability is reached, the training is done and a person can thereafter ride the horse through a small or big opening as the rider may wish. The animal dare not disobey the rider.

It is truly a major undertaking, is it not, for the Lord to train us who are such wild horses? Long are the hours He must spend to subdue even us. And what a wild horse loses after being trained by its master is the same as what we lose after we too have been trained by our Master—namely, our subjectivity. And the horse becomes so trained that it can now sense the slightest movement of the one who rides it. It will thereafter run as ordered. A similar result is what God is after with us.

"I will instruct thee and teach thee in the way which thou shalt go: I will counsel thee with mine eye upon thee. Be ye not as the horse, or as the mule, which have no understanding; whose trappings must be bit and bridle to hold them in, else they will not come near unto thee" (Ps. 32.8-9). How meaningful are these words. Given our higher place in God's creation, we humans ought to be much better than a horse or a mule. The latter, which have no understanding, can be so trained as to follow precisely the wish of the rider. How much more swiftly God's children ought to follow the wish and the leading of the Lord. A horse so trained is nevertheless termed as being without understanding because it requires a bit or a pull on the reins to know its master's mind. We, on the other hand, are able to look into the Lord's eye, something which cannot be done towards its master by a horse void of understanding. The psalm of David reads: "I will counsel thee with mine eye upon thee." As the Lord's eye moves, we who are sensitive and not subjective can know immediately. Before ever His hand moves, His eye has already moved, and we who are teachable have noticed it. The emphasis here is on the Master's *eye*, not His hand. How helpless, though, are the subjective ones!

Let us never imagine that man's nature and constitution are of no consequence to spiritual life. If you are subjective in living, you cannot be objective towards God; and thus you will not be able to know His will quickly. We may be satisfied with being simply a horse or a mule, but God is not satisfied with that at all. He will work until we will go where His eye looks. We are aware of His will in both moving and stopping. But if a person has his own idea and opinion, he is so subjective that it is impossible for him to wait for the Spirit of the Lord to indicate movement or cessation. Many times the Lord wants you to stop, but you cannot because you have injected yourself into God's will. One who *seeks* the Lord's will must leave himself out; and he who *does* the Lord's will also needs to put his self away. Then he is able to move or to stop at the Lord's command. Otherwise, being subjective, he will follow his own self. Hence many of God's people have this double problem: at the inauguration of God's will, they cannot begin to move; but similarly, once they are in the continuation of that will, they cannot stop. The greatest difficulty lies in our subjectivity: it is not easy for the will of God to be manifested in our lives.

To know the divine will is not a matter of method but is a matter of the person. No one is able to know God's will simply by being taught about its method. Only a right person using the right method will know. A wrong person with a right method will never know. Hence knowing the will of God hinges on the kind of person rather than the sort of method. One must not conclude from this that there is not method involved in knowing God's will. We merely stress that the person is all-important in the knowing of the divine will. For one may learn all the methods but still be ignorant of God's will because he is a wrong person. One needs to have his subjectivity broken by the Lord and become a person without preconceived ideas and opinions. And then, as soon as God begins to move, he instantly responds. Yet if he is not tender enough to move and to stop at God's command, he will neither know the will of God nor can he be His servant. A truly faithful and obedient servant of the Lord can be turned around by Him under any circumstance. However severe the outside demand is, it does not concern him. So that a basic requirement God looks for in a worker is the ability to be led effortlessly by Him.

Five

We must mention still another point on this subject. Only the person whose subjectivity has been dealt with by God is able to deal with other people. He will be led of the Lord to help others in following the will of God. The Lord cannot and does not trust a subjective person, simply because such an individual does not himself do the Lord's will. For were he to participate in the work of edifying brothers and sisters, he would lead them with one part of God's will and nine parts of his own will. A subjective person wants people to listen to *him*, not to God. Unless he is brought to the point of having no desire for others to hear him, he cannot be a useful servant of the Most High. How we need to be so broken by God that we never intend to have anyone hear *our* word. We will not interfere with another's business. We will not meddle with their lives and views. We have no intention of tampering with anyone's affairs. He who serves God must be brought to *this* point before he can be used by Him to represent His authority and to speak for Him. Otherwise, serious consequences will ensue, since despite the fact that God's authority would rest upon him he would nonetheless push forward his own idea. He himself would stand as the ruler or master or father to the children of God. "Ye know that the rulers of the Gentiles lord it over them, and their great ones exercise authority over them. Not so shall it be among you" (Matt. 20.25–26). How can God possibly use one who is unbroken, or full of his own secret desires? He is totally untrustworthy. If the Lord should ever commit His sheep to him, the latter would take them to his home. Such a subjective person is set in his own way; and therefore, he is in no way able to lead others to God.

Our brother Paul was so flexible. He himself was a celibate, and he realized that before God it was better to remain single than to be married; yet he never despised marriage. Do let us see how disciplined is our brother Paul in comparison with a person whose subjectivity has not been broken. If the latter were in Paul's position, he would persuade and cajole or perhaps even attempt to coerce all brothers and sisters to become celibate as he is and would even denounce all the married ones as being evil! A highly subjective person could easily do such a thing. Here, however, is a man who is so different. Paul could stand steadfast in his heart and know the value of his celibacy, yet he could also grant to others the liberty to walk differently. He wished for others to be spared the tribulation in the flesh that marriage brings; nevertheless he approved of people being married (see 1 Cor. 7.8-9, 28). Here was a man who was strong before God, and yet he was also tender—so much so, that later on, when some forbade marriage, he condemned this as a doctrine of demons (see 1 Tim. 4.1,3a).

Just here we all need to learn to stand on this ground that Paul had learned to stand on. We must not push a truth too far or, contrarily, remain quiet—because of our personal feeling—about a truth that needs to be presented or defended. Whenever our own feeling does not decide God's truth we may lead people to follow the Lord. So that the fundamental requirement is to have our subjectivity totally broken before God. In case we are strongly subjective, acting and speaking according to our own feeling, it will be hard to imagine the consequence to the work which God has entrusted to us. It will be a terrible thing. Instead, we must learn not to control people, nor interfere with others by interjecting our own subjectivity, nor violate their free will.

God planted the tree of the knowledge of good and evil in the Garden of Eden, and then He said: "thou shalt not eat of it"; but at this moment He did not surround it and the Garden, as He did later, with the flaming sword to keep man away. Had God done so, man would have never had the freedom, if he so desired, to sin. God could easily have done this, but He would not.

Instead, He warned man by saying: "of the tree of the knowledge of good and evil, thou shalt not eat of it: for in the day that thou eatest thereof thou shalt surely die" (Gen. 2.17). It was left up to man to eat or not to eat of this tree.

Like God Almighty (who could easily have coerced man), we must learn not to force our ideas and opinions upon other people. Whenever our words are not accepted, we should withdraw instead of pressing them further. If you have a burden before God, you should deliver it to the brothers and sisters. If they listen, fine; if they do not listen, you must drop it. Never try to compel them to take up your idea. For since God has never done it, we too must not do it. If people want to rebel, let them do so. If they do not wish to hear, why do you impel them to do otherwise? You need to learn not to force people and to learn to grant them the freedom not to listen to you. If you have indeed learned this lesson, you will naturally yield.

Hence, we do not compel people to hear us nor do we force them to accept our idea. We do not even coerce them to receive our help. Though we are aware of our ministry, we will not compel them to accept our help. God never forces anybody, and so we too do not force anyone.

There must not be subjectivity in the work of the Lord. Never try to make everyone listen to you. Learn to be careful before the Lord. The more people listen to you, the greater becomes your responsibility. Even greater will be your responsibility if you should speak wrongly and they listen. If people are willing to hear you, and your way is not straight and your understanding of God's will is not clear, then this will be like the blind leading the blind — and both will fall into the pit! Do not think that the follower alone falls and that you as the leader can save yourself. You cannot talk and teach cheaply, because you as well as those whom you teach will fall into the pit. Learn, therefore, to fear the Lord. Be aware that the more people listen to you, the more you must speak the word of God with fear and trembling. If you are 120 percent sure before God, speak only 70 or 80 percent, for fear that you just may be wrong. The more easily you speak heavy words the less weight you have before God. The more you are self-confident, the less you are trustworthy.

Never consider it to be too good a thing that people listen to you. For what will you do with them if they do listen to you? Where will you lead them? You ought to see the gravity of your responsibility and learn not to be subjective. Here, the problem with subjectivity lies in your wish that people hear you. You may take delight in making *your* idea and opinion the direction and light of other people. Let it be clearly acknowledged by you that *your* idea is not to be the direction of others, nor *your* opinion to be their light. Humbly learn not to drag people along your way, nor to pressure them to follow you or even to obey the Lord. If brothers and sisters are willing to walk with you, thank God. But when they want to choose their own way, let them so choose. We must not entertain the thought of grasping hold of them to follow us. Let them come and go as they wish. One true characteristic of a man who knows God is that he has no thought of forcing people to listen to or follow him.

A subjective person, however, is not like this. He is unable to listen to other people, nor can he receive guidance from God. He has not learned anything, and the Lord cannot trust him with His work. If everything has already been decided, how can any seek out God's decision? The tender-hearted and teachable alone may find God's decision. It takes our laying down of ourselves to know where the will of the Lord is. If the work of the Lord is given to a subjective person who has not learned to set aside his own opinion, way, idea, and doctrine, the Church will soon be split. The dividing into sects is actually built on man's subjectivity. Many are able to do their own works, but they are not able to do God's work. They know *personal* ministry but not the ministry of the *body*. They have never met authority; therefore, they could never be delegated authority. Oh how many there are who from the beginning of their service to the present moment have never submitted to anyone else. Naturally, they cannot be set up by God to represent authority.

Just here, there is one thing we need to watch carefully. When a young brother or sister commences to serve, give him or her a test. A subjective person always prefers to be his own head as well as that of others. He will naturally press his idea upon people. But one who has been dealt with by God has a special characteristic. He is not one to be unfaithful or to keep silent; he is faithful and he speaks, but he never forces people to accept his thought. On the one hand he is stable before God, on the other hand he is not subjective. Everybody has the freedom to obey or disobey God. We cannot compel anyone to do any thing. Each per-

son has his own responsibility before the Lord and
he must therefore learn to give people opportunity to
choose. May we become tender and flexible, always
allowing others to make their own choice. We simply
place the pathway before men to consider. May we
always ask, "What will you choose?" It is up to them
to choose the right way. Let us learn never to choose
for others.

Six

The subjectivity of a person can be detected in the
smallest of things, for it is a natural habit. If you have
learned the essential lesson of having your subjectivity broken, you will easily discern it in many small
details of life. A subjective person is that way in all
things. He loves to control people; he delights in being
opinionated; he takes pleasure in giving orders. He
knows what to do in every situation and circumstance.
When a young person steps out to serve the Lord, put
him together with a few other people, and soon you
will see whether or not he is subjective. If he is alone
in one place, you are not apt to find out. But when two
people are put together, you see at once that the subjective person will try to dominate the other. He will
insist on eating certain things, wearing clothing in a certain way, and sleeping at a certain hour. He is omniscient and omnipotent. Put two sisters in one room,
and you will discern which sister, if either, is subjective. Put two subjective people together, and they will
come to an impasse. One such person may live peacefully, but two such people cannot live on together.

This does not mean, however, that hereafter we should not say anything. When there is difficulty in the work or a problem with people, we cannot be unfaithful by remaining aloof. What we mean is that after we have spoken, we will not force them to adhere. If they do not listen after we have spoken, we will not feel hurt. So precious and dear to themselves are the opinions of some people that they are hurt if they are not listened to. Such is the feeling of subjective people. Yet, for the sake of faithfulness, we have to speak out. To speak out, though, is not to be construed as signifying that the person doing the speaking is a busybody or that he has a talkative temperament. But for those who are subjective, it is wrong to speak without first having been taught. God has not appointed us to be masters of all. Some have the habit of always speaking or teaching in every situation. This plainly indicates that one is a subjective person. Unless his kind of temperament is broken, he is not fit to work for God.

A subjective person is not necessarily a faithful person. One who is faithful speaks only when it is needed and not because he likes to speak or has the lust for talking. He speaks in order to rescue people from error. If he is rejected, he is not distressed since he is also able to remain quiet. Not so, however, with a subjective person, because having the lust to speak out on all occasions, he feels troubled if he does not speak. Have you ever noticed that a subjective person speaks out of his talkativeness? He simply loves to place his opinion upon other people. His idea becomes a yoke to others. He wants them to listen to him. He feels outraged if his opinion is ignored.

A subjective person and a faithful person are totally different from each other. We should be faithful. Many times it is wrong for us to keep quiet. Nevertheless, we must distinguish between faithfulness and subjectivity. The latter kind of person loves to meddle in others' business. He wants people to listen to him. He tries to control others. *His* way is always the first and the best. *His* way is most correct; therefore, everybody should walk in it. He cannot tolerate differences. Let it be known that the smallest person in the world is the subjective person. Only after one's subjectivity has been dealt with by God can he become a big man, so big that he is able to tolerate differences. Subjectivity is uniformity; it cannot bear any differences. That is why there will be no peace if two subjective people are put into one room. Each has his own idea, so the room will be full of strife. Each feels he is bearing the other's cross.

Be aware that a subjective person tends to take things into his hands and set himself up as the leader of God's people. He will decide everything for them. He has the habit of interfering in the smallest matters, and he likes to control everything. Because of this basic flaw, God will not commit himself to such people. We have never seen Him do so to such ones for He cannot use them. Nor have we ever seen any subjective person walk deeply in the Lord, simply because he has an unteachable temperament.

Because a subjective person is opinionated and always meddling in other men's affairs, this constitutes a great difficulty in the work of the Lord. He cannot learn, hence God cannot trust him. He expends all his energy on his subjective lifestyle so that there is no strength left to expend on God's work. When a person meddles in others' affairs, he neglects his own affairs. He tries to keep the vineyard of others but overlooks his own vineyard.

Let us acknowledge the fact that we really have no leisure time to be subjective. God has put into our hands enough ministries, responsibilities and concerns to care for so that we do not have the time to be busybodies. We need to concentrate our strength and time on performing that which we must finish. We are busy enough. Unless we forsake the work of God and leave our own responsibility, we will have no time to delve into the small affairs of others. This much is clear, that all who are subjective leave their own business undone that they might meddle in other men's business. How can we expect such a person to work well for God if he neglects his own work? A subjective person can therefore never do well in the Lord's work. The Lord cannot entrust anything to him since he will fail in every trust.

It is difficult to change one's subjectivity because it is a habit already formed and deeply ingrained. In his daily life, as we have seen, he is subjective in everything and at all times. He is not only this way in God's work, he is also this way in his daily concerns as well as in other men's affairs. A subjective man is truly the busiest person in the world inasmuch as he feels compelled to look after everything. He is not able to walk the straight path of God. In all matters— whether large or small—he has his idea, opinion and way. This becomes a hindrance to spirituality. We need to ask the Lord: "O Lord, be gracious to us that we may become tender and not be set in concrete before You and before our brothers and sisters."

Take a look at Paul one more time. "His letters, they say, are weighty and strong" (2 Cor. 10.10a). In truth, while he dealt with the testimony before God, his words *were* weighty and strong. But let us note how he was viewed by the Corinthians: "his bodily presence is weak, and his speech of no account" (2 Cor. 10.10b). Paul would not relax as it pertained to the testimony he kept, and hence his letters were weighty and strong. But when he met the Corinthians, he was perceived as being a tender and flexible person. We need to distinguish between our ministry, which is to be weighty and strong, and our personality, which must not be subjective. Some preach Christ out of good will. Let us thank God for that. Some, though, preach Christ out of envy and strife. Let us thank God as well. For in every way Christ is proclaimed; and hence, we should rejoice even as did Paul (see Phil. 1.15–18).

Do we see the balance here? We thank God if people, out of good will, want to walk with us; we are not distressed, however, if they prefer to go another way. Let us maintain this balance: faithful in testimony and not subjective in life. The faithful person is not subjective; yet the subjective person may not be faithful. These two are clearly distinguishable.

To sum up, then, subjectivity is nothing else but the manifestation of an unbroken self. We need to ask the Lord to break us so that we will not be subjective in the affairs of others as well as in our own matters. Once having been broken by the Lord we will become tender and flexible. Otherwise, if we lack this experience of brokenness, we will always remain more or less subjective. Some may be strongly subjective, others may be less so; nevertheless, in relation to others, there will always be—to one degree or another—imposed opinions, coercive methods, and attempts at control.

May the Lord deal with us drastically that we will not be able to stand on our own ground again. And once that happens we shall have the capacity to be faithful in testimony and to grant people the freedom to choose whether or not to listen to us. We will cease to speak on every occasion; we will cease to be teachers to so many people; and we will never force others to follow us. Let us ever be strong in ministry, but let us continually learn to be gentle in life. In short, we must not be subjective.

9 | A Right Attitude Towards Money

What should be the attitude of God's workman towards the issue of money? This is also an important feature of proper character for he cannot serve without passing this test. A worker has much opportunity to touch money. What can he do if he should fail here?

The fundamental concept of a Christian towards money is that Mammon (the Idol of Money, Wealth, or Riches) stands in opposition to God. It must therefore be rejected by the children of God. We must not fall under the influence of that which this idol represents. No worker who himself has not been delivered from the power of mammon is able to help or rescue other brothers and sisters out from under its influence. If we ourselves are controlled and bound by mammon, how can we ever set the others free from it? This is absolutely impossible. A worker should hate the influence of mammon as much as he should abhor laziness. Otherwise, he is of no use in God's work. Money or wealth is indeed a big problem. Let us mention a few things about money.

One

First, the relationship between the love of money and truth. We know of the character of Balaam in the Old Testament (see Num. 22–24). His way and his teaching are mentioned a number of times in the New Testament. They are recorded in one epistle of Peter, in the epistle of Jude, and also in the book of Revelation. This frequency thus evidences the serious attention God gives to Balaam's life and its pitfalls. Balaam was a prophet who ran for profit. In other words, his prophetic ministry was for sale.

Yet this was not because he did not know his position, for he certainly knew; nor was it because he did not know God's will, for he unquestionably knew that as well. When he first was asked to curse God's people, it was immediately made known to him by God that he could not curse them because the children of Israel were blessed by the Lord. But he was tempted by the reward Balak promised to give him, and so he nonetheless thereafter asked God again if he could go to Balak. Finally, God said go.

Many commit a fundamental error of calling this exercise a "waiting upon God." The fact of the matter was that had Balak not given him such a promise of reward (and in the prophet's mind, the promise made by Balak of promotion to "very great honor" included a "house full of silver and gold" — see Num. 22.17–18), Balaam would not have even inquired of God again, since he fully understood that doing Balak's bidding of cursing the Israelites was definitely not the Lord's will: God would bless instead of curse. Yet on account of Balak's promises, he inquired of the Lord once more. When God finally said, "go," this permission did not represent His will at all; rather, it was simply a case of God letting Balaam go to do as he wished. From the divine standpoint, God permitted Balaam to go because He who knows the hearts of all men knew that at the back of Balaam's much "prayer" was the influence of Balak's promised reward. Balaam was truly a prophet, but he was influenced by the love of money; and thus he went into error.

A person who has not been delivered from the power of money will invariably go where the money is. He will naturally look for a place where the supply is. In short, *supply* becomes the instrument of his guidance. He will not go to a poor place, and even if he does go, he will depart quickly. He will more naturally go to places of abundance. His footsteps are influenced by money supply, though he himself may interpret it to be God's leading. Supply is his primary attention. Profit and love of money caused Balaam to bother God again in asking for permission to go to such supply. Ten odd years ago, an elderly brother in the Lord lamented over this very situation, saying, "So many servants of God serve for money! So many poor places receive no care, while so many wealthy places are visited by many workers. Does this not indicate some problem in guidance?" These are weighty words.

It is not surprising that a brother who has not had the money issue solved in his life walks in the way of

Balaam. His path is directed by supply and how much the supply is. If a place is poor, he will either keep himself away or quickly leave after only a short visit. But if that place supplies much, he will frequently visit it or *even take up his residence there.* Since money has become his guidance, God can do nothing but let him go just as He did with Balaam long ago. A worker who is not independent of money is useless: he cannot be God's minister, for he will surely go the way of Balaam. And what is the way of Balaam? It is that path followed which is guided and influenced by mammon. May God give us grace that all of us will come out from under the influence, that none of us shall become "boarders" who allow the location where we serve to become our boarding-place because we are controlled by money.

How pitiful and how shameful it is for a servant of God to be guided and controlled by mammon! It is truly shameful if instead of seeking guidance before God we allow money to direct our footsteps. Unless we are absolutely delivered from the love of money, we will find ourselves under bondage to it when we seek for guidance. Indeed, to even mention the matter of money before God in relation to guidance is itself superfluous and certainly most odious. If the God who we believe in is living, we can go anywhere. If He is not living, we had better quit. What disgrace it is if we proclaim a living God and yet our way is governed by mammon!

In the New Testament, Peter, as we have indicated, mentioned the way of Balaam. He showed us in his second letter what the way of Balaam was. In the verse immediately preceding the one in which he speaks of Balaam, Peter wrote: "Having eyes full of adultery, and that cannot cease from sin; enticing unsteadfast souls; having a heart exercised in covetousness; children of cursing" (2.14). The emphasis here is on habit ("a heart exercised"), and the center of the problem is, of course, covetousness in the heart. Covetousness is habit-forming. After being greedy only a few times, it becomes a habit to covet. "Forsaking the right way, they went astray, having followed the way of Balaam, the son of Beor, who loved the hire of wrong-doing" (v.15). What will a person do who is habitually greedy? He will forsake the right way and follow the way of Balaam.

Yet God has *His* appointed way. Where ought we to walk? Some have forsaken the right way and followed Balaam's way. Balaam was a prophet who loved the hire of wrongdoing. His way was to sell his prophet ministry. The gospel is not for sale, nor is prophetic ministry for sale. We cannot sell God's gospel nor trade our ministry for gain. Here was a man who was willing to sell his prophetic ministry for gain. He had gone astray because his heart was exercised in covetousness; therefore, he went the wrong way as soon as he was tempted. His accepting Balak's call was not the first time he had become greedy, for his heart had been habitually exercised in covetousness.

Do we see the focus here? It is a matter of a habit of the heart. That was why as soon as Balak promised to give him "very great honor" in terms of "silver and gold" (see Num. 22.17–18,37b; 24.11,13), Balaam forsook the right way. All this demonstrates that unless the influence of mammon is completely uprooted and cleared out, it will tempt a person to follow its way. In order to walk straight and upright, we must thoroughly reject mammon. Otherwise, we will go astray in spite of the appearance of prayer and waiting on God. Balaam also prayed, waited and sought God; but he went the wrong way. Please be advised that if money still has a place in your heart and covetousness has become your habit, you will be governed by mammon and will not walk in the straight path even though you may have prayed many times seeking God's will.

The epistle of Jude also mentions Balaam. "Woe unto them! for they ... ran riotously in the error of Balaam for hire" (v.11). These are weighty words. Some run for profit. They run in a hurry in the error of Balaam. The error is that they run "for hire"—that is to say, they run for profit. Hence it is imperative that God's children be totally freed from the enticement of gain and profit, or else they will invariably hasten into error.

In 2 Peter 2, another phenomenon is mentioned besides the things concerning Balaam: "in covetousness shall they with feigned words make merchandise of you: whose sentence now from of old lingereth not, and their destruction slumbereth not" (v.3). In this particular chapter, Peter is speaking of false prophets. What do these false prophets do? Because of covetousness they exploit people with feigned words. Let us clearly understand that it is because of their covetousness that these false prophets and false teachers use feigned words to profit themselves at others' expense. If a person's way is governed by money, you will soon see that his teaching is also governed by that commodity. This is for sure. He will teach one thing to the poor and another thing to the rich. He will pronounce to the poor a certain demand of the Lord and pronounce to the rich some other requirement. His speech is influenced by his heart desire for profit. In other words, what he teaches follows the dictates of money. For this reason, the word of God concerning them is most frank and very weighty.

We are apprehensive that some will imitate these false prophets and false teachers. If anyone's way is swayed and altered by money, you know unmistakably that he is a false prophet or a false teacher. No prophet or teacher who serves God is to be under the influence of money whatsoever. If mammon can buy you who would seek to be God's workman and influence your way, you need to fall in dust and ashes and confess, "O Lord, I am a false prophet, I am a false teacher, I am a false servant. I do not really serve You." This matter is extremely grave. Man must be *fully* saved from mammon. Anyone who thinks of money supply in his way and teaching should be totally excluded from the work and service of God.

Paul wrote the same thing in his first epistle to Timothy as Peter and Jude had written in their epistles. He paid special attention to this matter as he conversed by letter with Timothy. He began the sixth chapter by saying: "If any man teacheth a different doctrine, and consenteth not to sound words, even the words of our Lord Jesus Christ, and to the doctrine which is according to godliness" (v.3). How would you describe such an errant man with those who keep the sound words of our Lord Jesus Christ? In answer, Paul would explain, as he did in the next verses, that "he is puffed up, knowing nothing, but doting about questionings and disputes of words, whereof cometh envy, strife, railings, evil surmisings, wranglings of men corrupted in mind and bereft of the truth, *supposing that godliness is a way of gain*" (vv.4–5). Here is a most amazing observation. In reading Church history, you cannot find anyone who taught a strange doctrine who was willing to spend and be spent for the gospel as had Paul. All who teach a different doctrine seek gain through what they teach. They calculate how much output will come out of so much input. We would fervently wish and hope that no preacher of the gospel would ever seek gain from anybody.

Nothing in the world is more condemned by God than using godliness as a way of gain. To make profit in that manner is most despicable. A workman must be washed clean of gain before he can ever touch God's work. If anyone truly desires to serve the Lord, he must be independent of money. Such a one would rather starve to death than expect to make profit. Every worker of God should be strong in this significant area of character-formation. Let us never give ground to anyone or anything that would tempt us in this matter. We need to follow the Lord strictly.

We may sell our clothes and other possessions, but we must never sell our doctrine and godliness. It is far better for us not to touch the Lord's work at all if we have never died to money. He who is unable to boast with Paul is unfit to serve as a workman for God. Paul's boast is just this, that "godliness with contentment is great gain" (v.6). Here is truly great gain. In godliness I am contented. Godliness is not asking or expecting anything. Godliness is contentment with what one has.

And this, said Paul, is gain, *great* gain. To use godliness as a means to make money is most shameful. But godliness with contentment is great gain. The very next words of Paul are especially worth being listened to and heeded by those who would be God's workers:

> For we brought nothing into the world, [and] neither can we carry anything out; but having food and covering we shall be therewith content. But they that are minded to be rich fall into a temptation and a snare and many foolish and hurtful lusts, such as drown men in destruction and perdition. For the love of money is a root of all kinds of evil: which some reaching after have been led astray from the faith, and have pierced themselves through with many sorrows. (vv.7–10)

We must never use godliness as a way to gain. We must be totally independent of money and its pernicious influence. If we should have any trouble here in resolving this issue, we had better find another job. We must not fall so low as to be led and guided by money and its consideration. If so, it would be better for us to serve God in one of the professions. None who seek to serve the Lord can be careless in the area of money; else he will disgrace the name of the Lord. Every workman must be clean in this money matter. His deliverance must be absolute, for being in any way unclear on this issue of mammon is most severely condemned in God's word.

The apostle Jude penned the following words: "These are murmurers, complainers, walking after their lusts (and their mouth speaketh great swelling words), showing respect of persons for the sake of advantage" (v.16). Many talk boastfully and arrogantly. They declare how many times their prayers have been answered and what great and astonishing miracles they have performed. They say these words for the sake of advantage. They flatter people, speaking words pleasant to the ears in order that they might make some gain. Oh, let us see that whoever is weak on the issue of money will be weak in everything else. In the matter of mammon, we should be strong, firm, and unyielding in resisting its influence if not its outright governance in our life and work. As those who would do the work of the Lord, we need to deal radically in this facet of our character-formation.

Two

The second thing we should mention in relation to money is to notice how the Lord Jesus trained His disciples. Luke 9 records the sending out of the twelve disciples; and Luke 10, the sending of the seventy disciples. Of the four Gospels, Luke is the only record we have of the sending out of the Seventy. When the Lord sent forth the Twelve, He spoke to them as follows: "Take nothing for your journey, neither staff, nor wallet, nor bread, nor money; neither have two coats" (Luke 9.3). The Lord told them not to bring these things with them. When He sent out the Seventy, He spoke to them in part as follows: "Carry no purse, no wallet, no shoes" (Luke 10.4). On this point He gave to both groups the same order as it pertained to money. In other words, when a person goes out to work, the consideration of money does not even exist. Significantly, later on, the

Lord asked them this: "When I sent you forth without purse, and wallet, and shoes, lacked ye anything?" And they answered, "Nothing" (Luke 22.35). He then followed this up by saying: "But now, he that hath a purse, let him take it, and likewise a wallet; and he that hath none, let him sell his cloak, and buy a sword" (v.36). This statement was now uttered because the time and circumstance had changed inasmuch as the Lord Jesus was already being rejected. But during the days when the Lord was accepted by the Israelites, the disciples had no need to carry these things.

The point which needs to be made today is that whenever someone is sent forth by the Lord, he should pay little if any attention to this issue of the purse. His entire being is devoted to the message, not at all to the purse. He goes forth to testify that Jesus of Nazareth is appointed by God to be Lord of all. He is committed to this message, not to the purse. In other words, he who goes out to serve has already come out from under money and its consideration. In order to go through villages and cities to proclaim the gospel of the kingdom, one must not be like a camel, unable himself to enter into the kingdom of God through a needle's eye, and yet encouraging other people to press hard into it themselves. This is simply impossible.

What is meant in Luke 9 by the phrase, "take nothing," or in Luke 10 by the phrase, "Do not carry"? It means that the principle of the gospel and that of purse and coats and shoes do not agree. When a man goes forth to proclaim the gospel, he is not anxious about these things. In normal traveling, a purse is for carrying money; a staff, for walking; and two coats, for a change of clothing; and these are necessary. And this is in keeping with Luke 22, where the Lord is recorded as saying: "let him take." Why, then, in the sending forth of the Twelve recorded in Luke 9 and in the sending out of the Seventy recorded in Luke 10, He said, "Take nothing"? In saying "take nothing" in these latter two instances He would want us to know that whoever today goes forth to preach the gospel takes no thought of these things. He goes today, if he is sent, disregarding whether he has one or two coats, a staff or no staff, a purse or no purse, a wallet or no wallet, shoes or no shoes. And this is preaching the gospel. Such was the training our Lord gave to the Seventy as well as to the Twelve.

Are we clear on this point? If we want to preach the gospel, we must not let these things become a problem; otherwise, it is better for us not to go in the first place. The gospel demands our total concentration, so much so that these physical matters—such as coat, purse, and staff—constitute no problem or consideration to us. The gospel is the only burden in our heart. Whether or not we are received by people, we must not fail to stand before God as glorious witnesses of the Lord. Hence the Lord said this: "into whatsoever house he shall enter, first say, Peace be to this house" (Luke 10.5). How lovely is this gesture. A worker is one who gives peace. He ought to keep his dignity in the presence of God. We may be poor, but we as servants of God must never lose our dignity.

But what if people do not receive you? The Lord's answer would be: "as many as receive you not, when ye depart from that city, shake off the dust from your feet for a testimony against them" (Luke 9.5). Do we see the dignity of God's servants? At being driven away, they are not agitated by their complaining that unfortunately they have entered the wrong house. Instead, they shake off the dust from their feet; that is to say, they would not even collect on their feet the dust of the city. Yes, God's servants maintain their dignity. Unless they are able to overcome in this respect, they are not able to do the Lord's work. For this reason, a worker needs to deal thoroughly with the money issue before God, for it is a serious matter indeed.

We may also see how the Lord Jesus trained the disciples with respect to money in the instance of feeding the five thousand and, again, the four thousand. On one occasion our Lord had been preaching to a great multitude. According to the account given by Matthew, there were present about five thousand men, not counting women and children. When the evening had about come, His disciples came to Him, saying, "The place is desert, and the time is already past; send the multitudes away, that they may go into the villages, and buy themselves food." But the Lord Jesus said to them, "Give ye them to eat" (14.15–16). The disciples were anxious for the Lord to send the multitudes away that they might buy food for themselves, but the Lord told His disciples to feed the people. One of the disciples heard it and became so frightened that he replied, "Two hundred shillings' worth of bread is not sufficient for them, that every one may take a little" (John 6.7). We see here that the disciples were calculating the cost. But the Lord said, "How many loaves have ye? go and see" (Mark 6.38a). When they finally came up with five loaves and two fishes and gave them to Jesus, the Lord, as we know, miraculously fed the multitudes till all were full.

Please understand that whoever considers the two hundred shillings cannot serve God. If money looms so large in your eyes, you cannot perform the Lord's work. What Jesus in effect showed His disciples here was that everyone who would do God's work must be a person ready to give ("Give ye them . . ."). If a person is touched by money, he will calculate whether it is worthwhile. A worker of the Lord needs to be delivered from the influence of money so that it has absolutely no power over him. During the three or so years of His earthly ministry, our Lord gave himself unreservedly to the Twelve in training them. He showed them how to spend and be spent. In God's work, there is no such thing as worthwhile or not. It is a gross mistake to look at divine work from a commercial viewpoint. He who calculates concerning money is not a servant of God, but a servant of Mammon. Let us therefore learn to get out from under the influence of money.

The disciples were unable, however, to learn this lesson at once. And hence, Matthew 15 tells us of the subsequent instance of the four thousand gathered together (excluding, again, the number of women and children who were also present). This occasion was more serious than the previous one, inasmuch as the multitude this time had already been present for three days when the Lord took action. What could these disciples do amidst such circumstances? The Lord said to them, "I have compassion on the multitude, because they continue with me now three days and have nothing to eat" (Matt. 15.32a). Not only the multitude, but the Lord too had nothing to eat. "I would not send them away fasting, lest haply they faint on the way," reasoned the Lord compassionately (v.32b). The disciples, though, had not yet learned the lesson from the feeding of the previous multitude. They inquired once again from whence bread for so many people could be obtained. Man's problem is where to get bread. "How many loaves have ye?" asked the Lord. "Seven, and a few small fishes," answered the disciples (v.34). After they brought out the seven loaves and the few small fishes, the Lord performed once more the miracle of feeding a huge gathering—this time the four thousand plus women and children.

The Lord performed this act twice, because, among other reasons, the disciples needed this double training. Suppose our Lord had not fed the five thousand and the four thousand; it is quite possible that the disciples would not have taken care of anyone after Pentecost. Whoever is ignorant of the events of the five thousand and four thousand in the Gospels may not be sympathetic towards the needs of the three thousand and five thousand recorded in the book of the Acts. By the same token, he who flees from the lion and the bear will also flee at the sight of Goliath, and anyone who does not take care of the sheep of the field will not take care of the children of Israel (cf. the life of David). Here were a group of people who had finally learned the lesson of the feeding of the five thousand and the four thousand. So that when the Day of Pentecost came, they had no problem in caring for the poor as represented by the three thousand on that Day, and later by the five thousand more.

For this reason we who would be the Lord's work-men all need to receive the same training from God. Our hearts need to be enlarged. We may be frugal ourselves, but God does not want us to conserve His miracle. Many are so tight in money that others may wonder whether they actually do the things the trained servants of the Lord should do. For the one truly trained by God, money is not a big issue in his heart, nor is money so tight in his hand. Let us acknowledge the fact that the more we calculate, the more we are wrong and the poorer we become. For such an attitude is not at all God's principle with respect to money. We need to receive the training the Twelve and the Seventy experienced.

Of the Twelve, nonetheless, there was one who was a thief. He stole from the common purse. He had not learned the lesson. Money was still a principle issue in his life. When finally he witnessed Mary breaking the alabaster flask and pouring the costly nard upon the Lord, he thought this to be a terrible waste and said so. "Why was not this ointment sold for three hundred shillings," he remonstrated, "and given to the poor?" But the Lord did not think in these terms. Instead, He offered these observations: "Verily I say unto you, Wheresoever this gospel shall be preached in the whole world, that also which this woman hath done shall be spoken of for a memorial of her" (Matt. 26.13). Break-ing the alabaster flask and pouring out the three hun-dred shillings' worth of costly ointment upon the Lord is the result, pure and simple, of the gospel. In other words, in the eyes of Jesus it is only proper and fitting for a person who has received the gospel to take no thought of cost nor to consider it a waste for such a thing to be done for His sake. Even if such an act would appear to be overspending a little or would be deemed a "waste" on behalf of the Lord, it would nonetheless still be right. Those who do *not* know the gospel are always calculating; but those who *do* know the gospel realize that such "waste" is quite fitting. The Lord is worthy to receive the "waste" of all.

Let us take further cognizance of the one who declared the poured-out three hundred shillings' worth of perfume to be a waste. Judas Iscariot was a man who had not by this time learned the lesson. What he said does sound quite reasonable from the human perspective. According to man's estimate, expending three hundred shillings in one anointing act is not worth it! It pained Judas to the very center of his being to have had to witness such a "waste." He wished to take advantage of it. He was truly a calculating man. Yet a person who has really received and appreciated the gospel is willing to give all for the sake of the Lord. And if he seems to give too much, this too much is still fully in accord with the gospel. In no place where the gospel is received will there be any who will bargain with the Lord. "Ye have the poor always with you," noted Jesus; "but me ye have not always" (Matt. 26.11). What Jesus meant here is that while you must indeed take care of the poor, whatever you expend on Me is never considered a waste. No matter how much is done or spent on His behalf, it is not a waste.

A brother once made this telling observation: "People who remain moderate just after believing the Lord have little spiritual future." There will indeed be time for us to be moderate after ten or twenty years; but at the time you first believe you should "waste" a little on the Lord. If at the time of our first belief we lay out all, pouring out all the pure nard in the alabaster flask upon the Lord Jesus, we will find the way. This was the very education the disciples received. Let us learn to suffer a little ourselves but spend more on the Lord and on other people. The attitude of God's servants towards money must be drastic. They will go forth, money or no money. It is never right to bargain.

From Acts 3 we learn that Peter said to the man who was lame: "Silver and gold have I none" (v.6a). Both he and John were brought by the Lord to such a place that they had neither silver nor gold. Though in Acts chapter 2 verses 44 and 45 there was evidence of a substantial amount of wealth, in chapter 3 it is a different story, wherein we find Peter declaring: "Silver and gold have I none." Yet he did continue on to say: "but what I have, that give I thee. In the name of Jesus Christ of Nazareth, walk" (v.6b). Large sums of money had indeed passed through their hands, yet they had neither silver nor gold. Peter and John had learned their lessons well by this time.

If anyone is engaged in the work of God, he must be strong in relation to this matter of mammon. Weakness *here* means weakness *everywhere*. A primary reason why one is strong and unwavering in the work of the Lord is the fact that he is trustworthy in the tempting area of money. And if he is found trustworthy here, he can be trusted by God.

Three

Let us look at a third facet of this issue as revealed to us by *Paul's* attitude towards money. He expressed himself very clearly on this. On the occasion when he spoke to the Ephesian elders assembled at Miletus, Paul declared unequivocally: "I coveted no man's silver, or gold, or apparel" (Acts 20.33). This showed he had no greediness in his heart. On the one side, he was able to testify that in working for God he had absolutely no thought of gaining to himself anyone's silver, gold, or apparel. On the other side, Paul could also state this: "Ye yourselves know that these hands ministered unto my necessities, and to them that were with me" (v.34). This is to be the two-fold attitude every servant of God must have. We should be able to say before God (1) that we have not coveted anyone's silver, gold, or apparel: the things which belong to you we do not desire and you should keep them; and (2) that we are willing to work with our hands to supply the needs of our fellow-workers and ourselves. Yet this two-fold attitude does not mean that those who serve the Lord cannot exercise their right which they legitimately have in the gospel to receive support from those among whom they minister (see Matt. 10.10b; Luke 10.7b; 1 Cor. 9.1–14; 1 Tim. 5.18). It simply means that they have such a sense of duty towards the gospel that they are ready to invest their hands, time, energy, and money into it. We all need to have such a heart wish before God. Let these two hands of mine work. Though Paul did indeed receive people's gifts, this was the responsibility of others; and that aspect will be touched upon further on in our discussion.

How well Paul spoke to the Corinthians:

> Or did I commit a sin in abasing myself that ye might be exalted, because I preached to you the gospel of God for nought? ... and when I was present with you and was in want, I was not a burden on any man; for the brethren, when they came from Macedonia, supplied the measure of my want; and in everything I kept myself from being burdensome unto you, and so will I keep myself. As the truth of Christ is in me, no man shall stop me of this glorying in the regions of Achaia. Wherefore? because I love you not? God knoweth. But what I do, that I will do, that I may cut off occasion from them that desire an occasion; that wherein they glory, they may be found even as we. (2 Cor. 11.7, 9–12).

Paul was not refusing any gift from elsewhere (in this case, from the Philippians and others in Macedonia); he merely declared that in the regions of Achaia (where Corinth was located) he would not receive anything. This was for the sake of the testimony, for he would not give opportunity to those who sought to vilify him to boast in themselves. He declared that he would preach the gospel of God to them without charge and that he would not be a burden to them, not even in time of his personal want. He would be careful now and forever in what he did. This was not because he did not love them. This was only done to cut off the claim of those who sought for an occasion to boast. Now this, may I say, is the proper attitude of a worker towards money which all who desire to be used of God as His servants should have.

Wherever we are, we must maintain this attitude so as not to give occasion for any slanderous word. In doing the Lord's work, the children of God must preserve their dignity. The more that people love money, the more we will preach the gospel to them without charge. The more they hold tightly to money, the less we will accept their contribution. Do we now see the position of a servant of God? In case you meet people like those in the regions of Achaia—who are reluctant to give yet seek occasion to speak against others—you should be like Paul, declaring as he did: "I will not be burdensome to you." Paul could forward the gift the Corinthians gave for the poor in Jerusalem. He could ask them to send forth Timothy peacefully. But as for Paul himself, he would maintain the dignity of a workman of God. If therefore you cause people to talk by accepting some gift, you lose the dignity that is yours of serving God. You ought to keep and preserve that dignity at all costs. You must not be lax on this money issue; otherwise, you are not able to do the work of God.

Paul showed us that besides keeping his own dignity, he also worked with his own hands to supply the needs of his fellow-workers. This exemplifies the principle of "giving"—even as Paul openly declared before the assembled Ephesian elders: "These hands ministered unto my necessities, and to them that were with me." Every worker must know how to give. If you keep all which comes in for yourself—whether food, clothing, money, or whatever—you do not know what the work of a minister is. The insufficiency of supply among fellow-workers today proves that there is some inade-

quacy somewhere in giving. A brother whose faith is
limited only to receiving has limited use in the work
of God.

Our spiritual future before God depends upon our
attitude towards money. The worst attitude a workman
can ever have is one of always and only giving to himself. Today it seems fairly difficult to get the Levites
to give; yet the Old Testament scriptures made quite
plain the fact that the Levites should also give their tithe.
True, the Levites had no inheritance in the cities, for
they lived among the twelve tribes of Israel. They lived
by the altar. Perhaps some Levite might have even said
in his day: "I live by the altar. What can I give?" Yet
God declared that all the Levites, who received the one-
tenth from the rest of Israel, had also to give *their* one-
tenth. This Old Testament record has been preserved
so as to remind all the "Levitical" servants of God today that they cannot excuse themselves from giving
simply because they have forsaken everything and
receive a very meagre income. If a person should always
and only look out for his own need, he will have no
way of supplying his fellow-workers. No, according to
our ability, we should be able to supply all the other
brothers and sisters in the work. In the event we hold
back our money and other material resources, regardless
the total amount, and expect the Lord to move another
brother or sister to give, we will not be entrusted with
money by God. How well Paul has spoken with respect
to himself and those in the work with him: "as poor,
yet making many rich" (2 Cor. 6.10b). Here was a
brother who knew God. He seemed to be poor, and yet

strangely he and those workers with him made many others rich. Our way together can be no less than this.

If you go out to work and discover that some in the Church have spoken something against you or have shown a wrong attitude towards you, you should preserve the dignity of a worker and refuse to accept their gift. You should tell them plainly: "I cannot use your money. I am a man who serves God. Because there are adverse words among you, I cannot take your money. I must maintain the glory of God." Even if you are poor, you must still learn to give. To receive more, you must give more. The more you give, the more you shall receive. This is a spiritual principle that runs throughout God's word. Many a time when we are in lack, we try our best to give. And after the money gives out, the Lord's supply comes in. Some brothers and sisters have had enough experience to testify to the truth of this. Never look at how much is left in your hand: "for with what measure ye mete it shall be measured to you again" (Luke 6.38c). Such is the law of God. We cannot break His law. Very different is the way we Christians manage money from the way the world manages it. They increase by *saving up*, whereas we increase by *giving out*. Though we are poor, we can still make many rich.

"Behold, this is the third time I am ready to come to you," said Paul; "and I will not be a burden to you" (2 Cor. 12.14). This was his attitude always. And how solemn it all was! There had been unwarranted words spoken against him during his former visits, so now in this impending third visit he was determined to continue not to be a burden to them. For, he explained, "I seek not yours, but you." Was this an indication that his heart was straitened and his capacity small? Not at all. For he went on to say that "the children ought not to lay up for the parents, but the parents for the children."

Can we not see how very commendable was Paul's attitude here? Because the Corinthians had listened to many slanderous words about him, Paul felt he could not accept their gift. And yet he did not withdraw from them or refrain from instructing them on issues of money and other matters. It can be said with certitude that the matter of money is mentioned more extensively in this second letter to the Corinthians than in any other of his many letters. If he were not to mention the money matter (the contribution for the Jerusalem poor) to the Corinthians, this would be evidence that he had been hurt to the point of abandoning them. But money had no power over him. He was not hurt to the point of giving up on them; on the contrary, he was able to go forward without any bitterness and instruct the Corinthians concerning the money issue. Paul told them they should send a contribution to Jerusalem; he did not tell them not to send. Paul rose so high above mammon that he was not affected by the attitude of the Corinthians towards him.

In spite of the fact that he must keep his dignity by refusing the gift to himself from the Corinthians, he could yet recommend these same Corinthians in Achaia to the Macedonians, declaring: "Achaia hath been prepared for a year past." He thought, however, that in case the Corinthians in Achaia were found unprepared when the Macedonians came into their midst and he (as well as the Corinthians themselves) would thus be put to shame, he would now urge them to be ready (2 Cor. 9.2,4-5). His own personal feeling was not at all involved here.

Truly, this servant of God had to be one who had been delivered from money, or else the Corinthians would not have heard or listened to this message. In the circumstances, Paul could very well have communicated these words to the Ephesians and to the Philippians but refrained from imparting them to the Corinthians. But to the latter he gave the very same words. He did not let up. He deemed it imperative that he talk to the Corinthians about money, for what he aimed at was that at least God could use their gift even if he could not and would not use it. He would not seek anything for himself, and at the same time in this matter of supply he would not be a burden to them. Nevertheless, he still expected the Corinthians to walk uprightly before God.

Let us look further into Paul's unique statement, "I seek not yours, but you." Each time you who are God's servants are in touch with brothers and sisters in the Church, are you able to distinguish between "you" and "yours?" Do you seek for "them" or "theirs?" Suppose you could not have "theirs" because they had questioned your sincerity; would you still support them, edify them, and expect them to grow? Paul had sufficient grounds to reject the Corinthians, but he nonetheless continued to visit them, even doing so for the *third* time. And why? Because he sought "them," not "theirs." This is in fact one of the greatest temptations to the servants of God. Let us learn to do and to conduct ourselves even as Paul did.

Furthermore, the apostle mentioned something else to the Corinthians:

> I will most gladly spend and be spent for your souls. If I love you more abundantly, am I loved the less? But be it so, I did not myself burden you ... Did I take advantage of you by any one of them whom I have sent unto you? I exhorted Titus, and I sent the brother with him. Did Titus take any advantage of you? walked we not in the same spirit? walked we not in the same steps? (2 Cor. 12.15–18)

Behold Paul's attitude here. How willing he was to spend and be spent for the Corinthians. In preaching the gospel, not only the person himself but also all that he has must be fully committed. How wrong it is to collect money through the preaching of the gospel. Let us be prepared instead to cast in our portion as well. We are not trustworthy workmen if we keep back our money. Paul was willing to spend himself and his all for the souls of the Corinthians, and he in addition would not be a financial or material burden to them. Neither Titus nor the other brother whom Paul sent was to be burdensome either. Paul would not take advantage of anybody. The gospel is glorious, so we must use our own money also in preaching it. Let us be like the apostle that we shall not be burdensome to anyone. Let us spend and be spent for the sake of the gospel. Then we will be on the right path.

On the other hand, let us carefully notice that Paul *did* receive those gifts sent him by the Macedonians and the Philippians. We therefore can conclude from this that it is proper for a preacher of the gospel to receive a gift under *normal* circumstances. Paul received from some and rejected from others. He would accept the gift of the Macedonians, for the latter had no misgivings about him. But in the regions of Achaia, the Corinthians sought occasion to criticize and defame him; so he would not take their gift. This was Paul's way. Today we should act the same. We may accept in some places, as in the case of Macedonia; but refuse in other places, as with the regions of Achaia where Corinth was. Let us see that we must faithfully heed this rule laid down by Paul's experience that not all money and gifts are acceptable. If there is criticism at the back, then we must not accept a certain gift proffered in this place or that. Yet in other places we may accept gifts.

Let us next read from Paul's letter to the Philippians to see how we should accept such a gift.

> Ye yourselves also know, ye Philippians, that in the beginning of the gospel, when I departed from Macedonia, no church had fellowship with me in the matter of giving and receiving but ye only; for even in Thessalonica ye sent once and again unto my need. Not that I seek for the gift; but I seek for the fruit that increaseth to your account. (Phil. 4.15–17)

Such was Paul's attitude. The Philippian church seemed to be the only one that sent Paul gifts. When he was in Corinth and in Thessalonica, it was the Philippians who remembered him. Yet he said to the latter: "Not that I seek for the gift; but I seek for the fruit that increaseth to your account." He knew that God would take into account the money sent and remember that this had been done by the Philippians. Here was a man who had such a beautiful attitude towards the only people who supplied his needs. These Macedonians in Philippi sent once and twice. Nevertheless, even as Paul made clear in his own experience, we must not be occupied with the money or material gift sent to us. We may not accept every gift proffered to us; but even if we do accept, our primary attitude should be that we expect increase to the givers' account before God. Let me say once again that a servant of God who is not delivered in this matter of money shall be prone to err in all other matters.

"But," continued Paul, "I have all things, and abound" (Phil. 4.18a). How different is this report from ordinary ones. Usually in a report we will mention how much we still lack so that people will give or give more. But our brother Paul reported to the only local church that gave to him, on this wise: "I have all things, and abound." Notice the attitude of our brother. He said emphatically that he had all things and abounded. He had received enough from them, and termed their already delivered gift (at the hands of his helper Epaphroditus) as "an odor of a sweet smell, a sacrifice acceptable, well-pleasing to God" (v.18b). How lovely was the spirit of Paul. He was a man who had no attachment to money whatsoever. Money did not stir up any sensation in him.

Another most precious word, in this case a blessing, came forth from Paul: "And my God shall supply every need of yours according to his riches in glory in Christ Jesus" (v.19). He was grateful to them for their gift, yet he did not lose any of his dignity. Their gift had been offered as a sacrifice to God, not to Paul himself. So that it had no relationship to him. Nonetheless, he gave them the above-quoted blessing in return. All this caused Paul to offer up by way of conclusion the following doxology of praise and worship: "Now unto our God and Father be the glory for ever and ever. Amen" (v.20).

Four

Fourth and finally, let us mention a concluding aspect of our discussion on money. And here we would wish to examine Paul's attitude in managing the contribution of the various local churches for the Jerusalem poor that was eventually collected and sent forward through him.

> Moreover, brethren, we make known to you the grace of God which hath been given in the churches of Macedonia; how that in much proof of affliction the abundance of their joy and their deep poverty abounded unto the riches of their liberality. For according to their power, I bear witness, yea and beyond their power, they gave of their own accord, beseeching us with much entreaty in regard to this grace and the fellowship in the ministering to the saints. (2 Cor. 8.1-4)

Here is a point the children of God must grasp hold of. Especially should this be the attitude of God's workman as touching money in any place. The brethren in Macedonia (particularly the church at Philippi) gave when they heard from Paul about the famine in Jerusalem. Although they themselves were in much affliction and deep poverty, they gave beyond their power in order to care for the brethren in Jerusalem. What did they do? They pleaded with much entreaty for permission to participate in the grace and fellowship of ministering to the needy saints. In total disregard of their own suffering and poverty, they themselves wanted to have a part in this matter nonetheless. For this, they begged Paul insistently. In other words, Paul had not permitted them to do so upon their first request, for he was well aware of their straitened state. And this was the proper attitude which the apostle exhibited. One who works for the Lord does not take in money as soon as it becomes available, even though the gift is not for his own use. True, the brethren in Jerusalem had need, but this was not simply a matter of collecting money for them. Especially in the case of the Macedonians who were in such a distressful situation, it was only right not to accept their money. But they came back again and again, begging Paul for the favor and the fellowship of contributing to this ministration for the needy saints elsewhere.

Was not the attitude of both Paul and the Macedonians most commendable here? This is truly Christian. On the side of the givers, they will say this: "However poor and needy we are, we want to give beyond our power." And on the side of the brother who serves God, he will say this: "You need not give." How very gracious all this is! Later on, though, the servant-worker might say this: "If you really and truly want to give, I cannot forbid you." Paul knew how to manage church affairs. Although he saw the hardship of those in Jerusalem and was anxious to supply their need, his attitude was quite different from that of many modern-day workers.

Further on in this passage from 2 Corinthians 8 we read how Paul said this:

> Thanks be to God, who putteth the same earnest care for you into the heart of Titus. For he accepted indeed our exhortation; but being himself very earnest, he went forth unto you of his own accord. And we have sent together with him the brother ... to travel with us in the matter of this grace, which is ministered by us to the glory of the Lord, and to show our readiness: avoiding this, that any man should blame us in the matter of this bounty which is ministered by us; for we take thought for things honorable, not only in the sight of the Lord, but also in the sight of men. And we have sent with them our brother ... (vv.16–22)

Let us see what Paul did here. When he was entrusted with delivering the bounty to Jerusalem, he was most honorable in his way of handling it. No servant of God can be untidy in money matters. Paul would not allow anyone to blame him in this matter. He asked one brother, two brothers, nay even *three* brothers to take care of the money. He himself would not handle the money. What did the three brothers do? "We take thought for things honorable, not only in the sight of the Lord, but also in the sight of men." To avoid any problem or potential misunderstanding, it is better to have two or three men to manage the money of the Church.

Due to the seriousness of this matter of money, Paul purposely mentioned in his letters both to Timothy and Titus that an overseer should not be a lover of money (see 1 Tim. 3.3; Titus 1.7). Deacons should not be greedy for base gain either (see 1 Tim. 3.8). A brother who has not overcome in the area of money must not be an elder or a deacon. For this heart attitude of not being greedy in money constitutes one of the most fundamental qualifications for one to serve as an elder or a deacon. Peter said the same thing, he addressing it to those who were elders: "Tend the flock of God which is among you, exercising the oversight, not of constraint, but willingly, according to the will of God; nor yet for filthy lucre, but of a ready mind" (1 Peter 5.2). No one who is a lover of money can shepherd the flock of God.

May the Lord grant us grace that we may settle this issue of money in our hearts. If the love of money has not been dealt with, sooner or later this will cause untold serious problems. For this money matter is so basic to us that unless it is resolved we have no place in the work of God. Nothing can be solved if this remains unresolved. We must be independent of money. We must learn to refuse any gift given by places that illegitimately question our integrity as workmen of God. We must learn to bear the burdens of others by supplying the needs of our fellow-workers and fellow-believers as well as those of our own. We shall achieve much when we resolve on the Lord's side this issue of God and Mammon.

10 | Other Matters to Be Dealt With

By way of concluding our study on the character of God's workman we would like to mention some other matters which every one of the Lord's workers must deal with before God. These are: (1) maintaining the absoluteness of the truth, (2) caring for one's physical well-being, (3) not having undue concern about one's personal lifestyle, and (4) understanding such problem areas as virginity, marriage, and so forth.

One

A person who does the Lord's work must stand for the absoluteness of the truth. This naturally demands total deliverance from his own self. Many brothers and sisters are not completely loyal to the truth because they are affected by human relationships and their own emotions. Hence a basic requirement in the service of God is that truth must not be sacrificed. I can sacrifice myself and my emotions but not the truth. The difficulty with a number of workers lies in their concern about friends, acquaintances, relatives or families, and which in consequence may adversely affect their loyalty to the truth. God cannot use such people. For if truth be truth, nothing — not even one's own brother or relative or friend — can touch it.

Take, as an example, an instance in which the son of a worker asks for baptism. Realizing that this is a matter which concerns the truth, he should leave the case with the responsible brothers in the local church and let them decide if his son is ready for baptism. Many a time, however, the worker will take the position that his son is ready and should therefore be baptized. Thus a problem is caused due to this worker's lack of absoluteness towards the truth. He brings into the picture his father-and-son relationship. If he were truly absolute here, he would let such matters in the church be decided by the dictates of the truth. He would not act according to human relationship.

Another example can be given. If a strife should occur in any given assembly, people may be inclined to take sides according to their friendships or family relationships. They do not sit down, as they should, and weigh the absoluteness of the truth that is involved; instead, they follow the leading of their affection. This does not mean that they might *totally* neglect the truth, but it does show that they cannot be completely loyal towards it. To be absolute towards the truth in spiritual matters means that no personal feeling, friendship or human relationship can be allowed to influence the truth. For just as soon as human relationship comes into play, the truth shall no longer be upheld. Any addition of man's word diminishes the verity of God's word.

In the Bible there are recorded many decisions and commands of God which need continually to be proclaimed by His servants. We abhor the fact that there are those who are always proclaiming the impossible; but on the other hand, can anyone be a servant of God if he never preaches anything beyond his personal capability? Since the truth is absolute, no one should ever lower the word of the Lord because he himself has not reached that height. No one should alter God's word due to his own deficiency. On the contrary, sometimes you must speak ahead of what you are, far beyond your personal feeling or relationships. This is indeed a tremendous demand placed upon a servant of God. You cannot deal with your family members in one way and the other brothers and sisters in a different way. For the truth is absolute, and the Lord wants us to maintain its absolute character. Whatever God's word says must be equally applied to all people. You should not act differently because of any special relationship. To do so would be to lower the truth of God. This is not to say that were you to do so you would be *totally* untrue, but it *would* show that you were not being totally loyal towards the truth. Let us therefore learn to maintain this absoluteness. We must not compromise because of any human relationship. For we follow the truth, we do not follow man.

Many difficulties arise in the Church when the truth is sacrificed. Here, for instance, was how a division occurred in one local assembly: one brother said, "We had no intention of separating from you, but since you failed to inform us last night on a certain matter, we have now decided not to meet with you again." Yet the truth being absolute, it needs to be said to that brother that it really has nothing to do with his and the others with him being informed or not, because any separation that is perpetrated on that basis is automatically putting forward man in the place of truth.

Take as another example the case of how people at a certain place had expressed their desire to break bread separately. The reason given was that a brother asked a question at a meeting and it was not answered. Yet, whether one breaks bread together or separately must be a matter that is based on truth. If it is the latter, then it can have nothing to do with anyone's being well-treated or ill-treated.

Oh, let us understand most clearly that before we can serve God, this "self" of ours must be rooted out. If our keeping the word of God depends on the treatment we receive, we put ourselves ahead of divine truth. This comes about simply because we have pride and selfishness in us. We consider ourselves to be more important than the truth of God. How can we serve the Lord under such condition? In the way of God's service, we must totally deny our own selves. Whether we are pleased or hurt in a given situation is a consideration that is completely out of the question. It ought to make no difference how we feel or how we are treated. We cannot bend divine truth to follow our own feeling, for how boldly presumptuous we would be if we should cause God's truth to follow us!

We should see the glory of God's truth and never try to bring our personal feeling into it. How do we stand when compared with the truth of God? It is not that we are smaller than the truth, but that we are absolutely nothing in comparison to it. A tiny touch of self will most certainly damage the truth.

One brother happened to hear much criticism being leveled against a church assembly, but at first he considered it to be groundless. He subsequently paid a visit to that assembly. While in their midst, however, he touched only some of the brethren there without really touching the truth before God. He was actually quite careless in his conduct. One day, a brother in that assembly pointed out to him his earlier loose conduct based only on certain facts. This action by that brother was taken by his speaking the truth to him in love. Whereupon, he who had at first considered the earlier criticism of this church to be groundless now reacted by speaking disparagingly of this assembly. All this simply reveals the fact that this over-reacting brother was not absolute towards the truth; for had he *been* absolute, he would not have changed his attitude towards the church assembly in question simply because of the reprimand he had later received.

What is meant by the absoluteness of the truth? It means that no consideration of personal affection, relationship, experience or self-interest will intrude upon one's view and application of the truth. It means that none of these things is or can be involved in it. Since truth is absolute, yea is yea and nay is nay.

There was once a brother who had helped many people. He later walked in the way of maintaining the testimony of the church. Whether or not this way is right is not affected by the manner of his or anybody else's walk. His walking in this way of the testimony of the church does not make it right. Even if he should fall, this way is still right. And why? Because the truth is absolute. Unfortunately, the eyes of many were upon this brother. They simply assumed that he being right, that way must also be right. Or if he is wrong, that way must also be wrong. So what did they look at? At the truth or at the brother? It is obvious that it was the latter. Now, of course, this is not to suggest that anyone can be careless. We should indeed not be careless, for we must maintain the testimony of God. This is a fact. Even so, whether this way of the church is right or not is a matter to be judged by truth, not by man nor by the way man walks. Can we stop being Christians simply because some other Christians have sinned or fallen? Ought we to deny our faith merely because God's children are bad? Not so, for the truth is absolute. If the Lord is worth believing, we will believe in spite of the failure of fellow-believers. Though others may disbelieve, we will nonetheless believe. For the deter mination of the issue involved does not lie with the people but with the truth. The divisions in the Church and the many strifes in the work would all disappear if we would eliminate our personal feeling and relationship.

The absoluteness of the truth is not a small matter. We cannot afford to be loose here, because if we are lax in *this* matter, we will be lax in *all* matters. We shall be able to hold fast to the truth if we lay down ourselves; but without such a determination or habit before God, we shall sooner or later fall apart. Someone may thank the Lord for the helps he has received in a local church meeting. Yet this does not necessarily prove that he is clear about the absoluteness of the truth of the church and its testimony. Perhaps he only feels comfortable in that meeting. Wait, however, till he encounters something disagreeable to him; he may then feel quite differently about the meeting. Nevertheless, the truth still remains absolute. Whether or not the meeting is legitimate in his view should not depend on his treatment. If his treatment—whether good or ill—decides for him the legality of the meeting, then he becomes the most important person in the whole world! For in that case, truth is not important; he instead becomes most important. And consequently, he would not be absolute in his loyalty towards the truth. Herein lies much of the trouble in the Church.

God expects us to deal with ourselves to such a degree that we are able to set ourselves aside in any matter. In that event our personal feeling, pleasure or hurt will not create any difficulty. The direction of our course ahead is not to be governed by our personal feeling. If God says yea, it is yea; and if God says nay, it is nay. If He says this is the way, we will walk in it, even though no one else may so walk. We walk not because there is much excitement in the way, nor because some other brothers are walking in that way. We walk simply because this is the right way and the truth is held to be absolute. Nobody can be permitted to influence us, for if we allow anybody to do so, we shall then make this or that person bigger than the truth.

Judgment is also based on truth, and not on ourselves. If judgment should ever follow our personal taste, we shall have degraded the truth and the way of God. The foundation of God's judgment is the truth.

In judging any situation, we look not at the way people treat us but look exclusively at the truth of the Lord. In the work of the Lord, we never allow our personal feeling and interest to become involved. If truth commands separation, we will separate even from our best friends. Though we may daily eat together and live together, yet because of the absoluteness of the truth we will separate ourselves in spite of human affection. And by the same token, if the truth demands that we be together, then no matter how we brush and strive against each other we will still stay together. Should our being together be based on personal relationship, it is an indication that we do not know what the truth is. It will then be hard for us to finish the course set before us.

This that we have been discussing is a most fundamental issue. Our future depends on our learning the discipline of God. Truth will suffer at our hands if we regard ourselves as so big and important. In order to maintain the truth of the Lord, we ourselves must be set aside. Each one of us has his temperament and feeling. Let us not allow these to affect God's truth. No minister of the Lord can sacrifice or debase the truth of God to soothe his own feeling. If we disdain God's truth, we have no spiritual future before Him. A judge on the bench maintains an absolute attitude towards the law. He will pronounce guilty to the sinful and not guilty to the innocent. On the one hand, he cannot reckon the sinful as sinless simply because the latter might happen to be his brother or close friend. On the other hand, a judge cannot condemn a guiltless person merely because the latter happens to be his enemy.

Otherwise, these kinds of judgment would create disorder in society. A judge must therefore support the law. Similarly, we who believe in God and serve Him must support His truth and His law. No personal feeling is to be involved. May we never ever forget this point.

All of us need to be dealt with by the Lord. Let us say to Him, "Lord, I am nothing, but Your truth is everything." This being the case, there will be no difficulty in the work. If all fellow-workers can maintain the absoluteness of the truth there will in consequence be a great advantage, in that we can all speak frankly and things can be easily done. A matter that should be done will be done without the fear of incurring blame from other workers. What decides everything is the will of God. Is this His decision? If it is His will and He so desires, then we need not consider anything else. But if we do not see the truth as absolute, we shall find it difficult to move forward; because whenever something arises, all will be thinking what the others will say; with the result that we shall look for a compromise, and in the process the truth shall suffer because of us. Moreover, there shall be many words we will not dare to say and many matters we will not dare decide for fear of offending other people. And thus we shall find ourselves in great trouble.

Any church fellowship that supports the truth of God and rejects human politics is blessed. The brethren in such a fellowship as this do not play politics nor negotiate for a compromise. Quite the contrary, on the path of absoluteness in truth, all dare to speak and act as required: they look only at the will of God in their decision. Now if such in fact be the case there, that fellowship shall truly be blessed of the Lord. Otherwise, personal considerations will come, politics will be played, many compromising changes will occur, and the church local will no longer be the church.

All this needs to be carefully laid out before God, because this is a great and grave issue. No personal feeling and affection should be brought into the work. Even if you should be aware that your personal affection would be able to effect people's acceptance of the truth, you should still not bring it into the work. For instance, it would not be right for you to entertain a guest with a view to influencing him as to the truth, for although it might be a good will gesture on your part to give support to the truth in this manner, we believe the truth needs no human hand to support it since God's truth, being absolute, has a position, authority and power of its own. And therefore the truth does not require our help to advance its cause. We should therefore never be afraid that the truth, being rejected, is accordingly defeated; for in the end it shall prevail—and without any help on our part. Our responsibility is simply this: we must learn to respect God's truth, walk in the truth, and never compromise the truth. Amen.

Two

Another of these final matters is how a worker should take care of his body. We know Paul was a brother greatly gifted, and he often healed the sick through prayer. Still, he mentioned three persons whose sickness was never healed. One was Trophimus, a second was Timothy, and the third was himself.

When Trophimus was ill, Paul did not pray for his healing, nor did the apostle exercise his healing gift. He instead said, "Trophimus I left at Miletus sick" (2 Tim. 4.20a). Timothy had stomach trouble and was often ill. Again, Paul did not use his gift nor did he pray for healing. We know he healed many sick. So if he healed the others, why could he not heal Timothy? This younger servant of the Lord was to continue the work of Paul and was most useful, but Paul still did not heal the sickness of Timothy. For this thing was in the hand of God, not in Paul's hand. So what did the apostle say? "Be no longer a drinker of water, but use a little wine for thy stomach's sake and thine often infirmities" (1 Tim. 5.23). In other words, Timothy should take more care of himself: he should eat what was profitable to the body, and refrain from eating anything disagreeable: he should drink what would lessen the stomach trouble and not drink what would increase his trouble. These were the recommendations made by Paul to Timothy. And as for Paul himself, he had "a thorn in his flesh" for which he asked the Lord three times that it be removed. Yet the Lord did not see fit to heal him; He only said to him, "My grace is sufficient for thee" (2 Cor. 12.9a). Trophimus was left sick; Timothy was left with his stomach ailment and his other frequent infirmities; and Paul's thorn remained in his flesh.

It requires ten to twenty years for a person to be so trained by God as to be considerably useful. It really needs such a long period for one to be matured in the way of the Lord. But due to lack of knowledge in caring for the body, some may die before there is sufficient time for training. Or some may die just after they have touched the way of God and become truly useful after years of training before Him. All this is most regrettable.

In the churches, there should not be all children, or all young people. The churches need fathers. For this reason, all who learn to serve God must consider this matter of the care of the body. How sad if a brother or sister dies before reaching an appointed age after he or she has been trained for some time! We know many are cracked and broken at midway, just as sometimes clay becomes marred in the hands of the potter. As the potter turns his wheel, not all vessels come out to perfection bereft of any flaw. Some of the earthen vessels are marred in the making before they ever go through the fire. That is a loss. The Church loses many members because they cannot pass such testings. They fall as soon as they meet temptations. If by the mercy of God we are not marred or broken, we may still need the working of the cross in our lives to make us even more useful. A trial coming from the Lord may require a long time for us to get through. It may take a year or several years. The number of trials in the life of a child of God is rather limited. We do not have many opportunities to be tested. Many crack or break down at a time of trial and thus no good results from it. Not many of God's children come through trials triumphantly. Countless are those who collapse on the way! This is regrettable and it is a loss.

Of the six hundred thousand or so Israelites, only two living and two dead entered Canaan. Few lived on and crossed over. How very tragic it is that one should die just as the trial is nearly over! Now if this *should be* God's appointed time for us to die early, we have nothing to say. But if we mistreat our body, the work of God will suffer. For the Church to be truly rich spiritually, it needs to have among its people those of seventy, eighty and ninety years of age. If the Lord takes exception by calling one or two of His workers to himself early, we have nothing to say. But for us to be useful in the work, we should take a little more care of our body. One of the problems in the work of God is that just about the time that a person is almost trained his days on earth come to an end. Before any work is done, the body is already damaged. As soon as one begins to be used, he is gone to be with the Lord. How very sorrowful this is!

Therefore, let us not think it right to neglect our body. We do indeed need to have the mind to suffer and to buffet our body into obedience. Nevertheless, whenever possible, we must take care of our body. To be careless is easy; to be careful is not so easy. We need to learn to eat healthy food and in other ways take care of our body. There may be times when we must give our all if the Lord should so order and the work so demands. In ordinary days, though, we should learn to take care of the body according to the best way that men know.

Let us ever be mindful of this, that if we should lose even but one workman, we will lose ten to twenty years of the Lord's working in that person. There are not many tens or twenties of years in a lifetime. When one first commences to serve the Lord, he may have some gift, but he seldom has much use in ministry. To arrive at such usefulness in ministry, it will take him one or two decades. And this time estimate is only applicable to those who straitly walk in the way of the Lord. For people whose way is *not* straight, they may not arrive at usefulness even after this lengthy period. It is not a simple thing for God to spend twenty years to train a person. During those many years, he may need to be smitten and chiseled numerous times over by the Lord. It is not a light thing that a person who is to be useful must suffer, bear the cross, be smitten, and be under the disciplining hand of God—and not merely for one or two years, but for ten or twenty *long* years. If during this period he neglects his body, he will be gone before he reaches the time of greatest usefulness. How very sad and lamentable this is.

Once an elderly brother was asked: "To the best of your recollection, when would you say you have been the most useful throughout your life up to this point?" He thought for a while and replied: "The years between seventy and eighty." Truly, spiritual usefulness increases with age. The longer you are in the way of service, the more useful you become. We have noticed, unfortunately, that along this way some have died, some have become marred, some are broken, some have been of little use, while still others have been of no use. Very few reach their usefulness after twenty or thirty years of training, but by that time they are on the verge of departing from the world. This is really very, very sad! Yes, the more days one learns before God, the more useful he becomes. But for such a person to pass away prematurely is truly a regrettable event.

Now concerning the body more specifically, attention should be paid to preventive care as well as routine care. We readily acknowledge that we must not be lacking in our having the mind to suffer, and many a time we do indeed have to press on under the most difficult situations. Yet under *normal* conditions we shoud learn to take care of the body. We cannot afford to be careless in this matter.

As to the area of rest, we should do so at the time of rest. We are under such strain that sometimes we do not know how to relax in bed. If we are still tense there, we lose the value of sleep. We should learn to rest while sitting. A worker should be able to be tense when tension is required, but be able to relax during a few minutes of leisure. Otherwise, he will be tense all the time, which is certainly not good. We must learn how to relax.

During your leisure time you should relax your muscles. In sleep loosen your hands and feet. We as servants of God can be tense in time of need — more tense in fact than the strongest, for our body listens to us. But no one can be tense *all* the time. Our muscles and nerves need to be loosened up and rested. Many times we must make a conscious effort to find opportunity to rest in order that we may recover our equilibrium. Otherwise, we will cross the line of overwork and go to an extreme. Let us not be extremists here.

As in everything else we should learn to trust God for our body, and at the same time learn to rest as nature demands. We must learn how to relax. Then it will be easy for us to rest and go to sleep. According to the experience of some people, the number of breathings can help us in our sleeping. During sleep our breathing is deep. We cannot control the former, but we may control the latter. We may count our breathings. Let us learn to breathe slowly and long just as we breathe while actually at sleep. Yet let us not think of sleep, but think of breathing. Let us first engage in the sleep-like breathing, and then after a while the sleep will come. Many go to sleep using this very method. We believe God has created this body with a capacity for sleeping. We not only believe in God himself, we also believe in His creative laws. We need sleep, and we are able to sleep.

So try to loosen up your entire body in order that you may get some rest. If you cannot rest, you cannot help but be tense. And being tense both day and night, it will be impossible for you to do much work. Some may have infirmities, but if you learn to take better care of your body, you can spare it from a great deal of trouble.

The same is true with eating. In this area of concern, a worker should be on the lookout for nutrition, not for taste. He should eat more of the more nutritious food and eat less, or not eat at all, of the less nutritious food. We should also be careful not to over-eat and to learn to eat everything. Some brothers and sisters only eat those items which happen to fall within a narrow range of food. Such a habit is not good for the body. We need to eat broadly. Many varieties of food give nourishment to our body. If we eat only a few kinds of things, we may not feel any deficiency now, but we will surely discover its effect later in life. The length of one's life is influenced by the food he takes in.

Another benefit in eating broadly is the convenience

it gives to the worker. Otherwise, when you go out to work, you will create many problems if you refuse to take the food that is offered you. Naturally, of course, sickness is the one exception to this rule. But for ordinary situations, you should learn to eat all kinds of food. As the Lord Jesus himself said: "Eat such things as are set before you" (Luke 10.8). And this is indeed a good principle to follow.

Once on a ship a believer asked a fellow-believer, "Why did the Lord Jesus multiply the loaves *and* the fishes?" The answer given was: "The abundance of the sea adds to the abundance of the land." How well-phrased a statement this was. God's children should learn to eat the abundance of the sea as well as the abundance of the land. The scope of our food should be as broad as possible.

Do not deem this area of concern to be insignificant. If you do not deal with this matter, your health is bound to suffer. You should cause your body to listen to you. Though at the beginning there will be distress, for you may not like some foods, you must deal with this issue and learn to eat everything. You need, on the one hand, to have a mind to suffer, but on the other hand, you should learn to take care of your own body. We have no sympathy for those who do not take care of their body. Do not think hygiene to be an easy subject to talk about. To be hygienic is a more difficult task than to not be hygienic, for it requires self-control. Learn to eat nutritious food. Do not let your eating be governed by taste but by your bodily need. How can you neglect your body in the face of the fact that the Lord has spent many years on you? Pay attention to preventive hygiene. As much as the Lord permits you in your circumstances, do your best to comply with the requirements of your health. Take in whatever is profitable, and reject that which is harmful.

On the one hand, learn to deny self and be faithful unto death; on the other hand, unless the Lord orders differently, always preserve your own body. Wherever you go, try your best to be sanitary, but do not create a burden upon the brethren of that locality. Learn to trust God in the midst of an unsanitary environment. But under normal conditions pay attention to hygiene so that your body will not be damaged unnecessarily.

Three

There is yet another area of character-building which a worker for the Lord must consider. He must learn not to be obstinate in his lifestyle. A servant of God should never establish for himself an absolutely subjective standard of living; nor should he insist on having his own way. In order to serve God well, we must "become all things to all men" in accordance with the Biblical principle that is taught of not offending anyone. Paul wrote along this line as follows:

> Though I was free from all men, I brought myself under bondage to all, that I might gain the more. And to the Jews I became as a Jew, that I might gain Jews; to them that are under the law, as under the law, not being myself under the law, that I might gain them that are under the law; to them that are without law, as without law, not being without law to God, but under law to Christ, that I might gain

them that are without law. To the weak I became
weak, that I might gain the weak: I am become all
things to all men, that I may by all means save some.
(1 Cor. 9.19–22)

For the sake of the gospel, Paul became all things to
all men. Whoever serves the Lord should have this character trait.

In another place, the apostle also wrote this: "I know
how to be abased, and I know also how to abound: in
everything and in all things have I learned the secret
both to be filled and to be hungry, both to abound and
to be in want" (Phil. 4.12). It is easy for men to be lopsided, that is to say, easy for them to go to extreme.
For some, to be a Christian is to live in prosperity and
abundance; for others, to live in abasement, hunger and
want. Yet Paul said he had learned how to be abased
and how to abound, how to be filled and how to be
hungry. He had learned the secret in these things, which
was: "I can do all things in him that strengtheneth me"
(v.13). Thus was he able to accept any kind of life
condition.

Unfortunately some brothers and sisters are rather
obstinate in their daily life, so that their habits have
become absolutely unbreakable and unchangeable.
Some must always have warm water to wash the face;
others must be able to shave every day. If they go to
an environment where they cannot live according to
their normal way of life, they find it unbearable.
Although these matters may appear to be rather insignificant, they could verily hinder the work of the
Lord. People in such a state cannot be God's servants.
A worker should not be so firmly set in his daily habits

and routines; he should be able to wash with warm water or cold; he should be able to shave daily or go without shaving for one or two days; he should be able to change his shirt everyday or to wear the same shirt for days if need be; and he should be able to sleep on a hard bed or a soft bed. If a person is truly a servant of God he will be adaptable to all sorts of life conditions.

Temperament and age too should not become limitations to a workman of God. For example, in some places people are naturally warm and outgoing, whereas in some other places they may be temperamentally cool. A servant of God should be able to work among both these kinds of people. Suppose a worker's own temperament is rather on the cool side; if he can work only among those with a similar temperament but not work among those of a warm and outgoing sort, then the work of God will certainly suffer. We find, unfortunately, that some can work among the enthusiastic but not among the more quiet type, that some can work with the serious but not with the lighthearted. Such willful inclinations as these will limit the work of God. Then, too, some may be able to communicate well with the older people but have no rapport with young people or children. Such a lopsided disposition can circumscribe God's work. Let us not forget that our Lord received the elderly and blessed the little children. God wants us to be like Christ — receiving the older ones and blessing the young ones. It is not unlike what Madame Guyon once said when she remarked that a person wholly united with God can be the counsellor of the aged and the friend of little children. This adaptability is what we too need to adopt in our Christian lifestyle as servants of the Lord.

This all comes back, does it not, to the matter of dealing with our self life. Our self must be so broken that God can place us in any situation. We are to be neither obstinate, nor lopsided. Paul was able to be all things to all men because he had been dealt with by God. May we all receive such dealing so that our disposition and habit are no longer set in concrete or tilted in but one direction. In this way God's work will not be hindered or limited by us.

Four

One who does the Lord's work should also have a right understanding of, and appropriate solutions for, such matters as virginity, marriage and so forth. These issues are usually left undiscussed, but we feel the need to give some Biblical instruction on them because they are rather important in the life of a workman for God.

Concerning virginity, Paul gave definite instruction in 1 Corinthians 7:

> Now concerning virgins I have no commandment of the Lord: but I give my judgment, as one that hath obtained mercy of the Lord to be trustworthy. I think therefore that this is good by reason of the distress that is upon us, namely, that it is good for a man to be as he is. Art thou bound unto a wife? seek not to be loosed. Art thou loosed from a wife? seek not a wife. But shouldest thou marry, thou hast not sinned; and if a virgin marry, she hath not sinned. Yet such shall have tribulation in the flesh: and I would spare you. But this I say, brethren, the

time is shortened, that henceforth both those that
have wives may be as though they had none; and
those that weep, as though they wept not; and those
that rejoice, as though they rejoiced not; and those
that buy, as though they possessed not; and those
that use the world, as not using it to the full: for
the fashion of this world passeth away. But I would
have you to be free from cares. He that is unmar-
ried is careful for the things of the Lord, how he
may please the Lord: but he that is married is careful
for the things of the world, how he may please his
wife, and is divided. So also the woman that is un-
married and the virgin is careful for the things of
the Lord, that she may be holy both in body and
in spirit: but she that is married is careful for the
things of the world, how she may please her hus-
band. And this I say for your own profit; not that
I may cast a snare upon you, but for that which is
seemly, and that ye may attend upon the Lord without distraction. (vv.25–35)

Here we are shown that the benefit of virginity lies in
enabling a person to serve the Lord more diligently and
without distraction. In this respect, it does surpass those
ones who are with family.

Nevertheless, such a word is not for everyone. Let
us notice what then follows in Paul's discussion on these
issues:

But if any one think that he behaves unseemly to
his virginity, if he be beyond the flower of his age,
and so it must be, let him do what he will, he does
not sin: let them marry. But he who stands firm in
his heart, having no need, but has authority over
his own will, and has judged this in his heart to keep
his own virginity, he does well. So that he that mar-
ries himself does well; and he that does not marry

> does better. A wife is bound for whatever time her husband lives; but if the husband be fallen asleep, she is free to be married to whom she will, only in the Lord. But she is happier if she so remain, according to my judgment; but I think that I also have God's Spirit. (vv.36–40 Darby)

What is said here is plain enough. If anyone thinks he is not acting properly towards his own virginity, that he is passing the bloom of his youth and there is need for marriage, then let him do what to him seems right. To continue being single or not is a question for him to decide. Nobody else can choose for him. It is to be decided not only according to what he chooses in his heart but also according to his having need or no need. He has full authority over his own will.

In the Gospel of Matthew we find this passage:

> The disciples say unto him [Jesus], If the case of the man is so with his wife, it is not expedient to marry. But he said unto them, Not all men can receive this saying, but they to whom it is given. For there are eunuchs, that were so born from their mother's womb: and there are eunuchs, that were made eunuchs by men: and there are eunuchs, that made themselves eunuchs for the kingdom of heaven's sake. He that is able to receive it, let him receive it (19.10–12)

Joining the last clause of verse 11 with the last sentence of verse 12, we have this: "but they to whom it is given . . . He that is able to receive it, let him receive it." It is quite clear that to whom this word is given, let him receive it.

For the sake of having adequate time to serve the

Lord diligently without distraction, it is best to remain single. Among the disciples of our Lord, John was one who remained single. Paul, who came forth a short time later, was also single. Yet, should there be the need for marriage, let them be married: it is not a sin. The difference between marriage and virginity centers not on the matter of sin but on the consideration of time, diligence and distraction.

The body has been created by God, and all its needs have also been created by Him. Hence marriage is holy. But any bodily demand that is met outside of marriage is sinful in the eyes of the Lord. Why be married? To avoid any relationship outside of marriage. To be married is not only not a sin; it can serve as a prevention of sin. Marriage is not a moral fall; it prevents a fall.

Paul also spoke specifically on marriage in 1 Corinthians 7:

> Now concerning the things whereof ye wrote: It is good for a man not to touch a woman. But because of fornications, let each man have his own wife, and let each woman have her own husband. Let the husband render unto the wife her due: and likewise also the wife unto the husband. The wife hath not power over her own body, but the husband: and likewise also the husband hath not power over his own body, but the wife. Defraud ye not one the other, except it be by consent for a season, that ye may give yourselves unto prayer, and may be together again, that Satan tempt you not because of your incontinency. But this I say by way of concession, not of commandment. Yet I would that all men were even as I myself. Howbeit each man hath his own gift from God, one after this manner, and another after that.

> But I say to the unmarried and to widows, It is
> good for them if they abide even as I. But if they
> have not continency, let them marry: for it is better
> to marry than to burn.... (vv.1–9)

This passage points out that one of the purposes of marriage is to prevent fornication. At the same time it also reveals that some people are given a special gift from God so that they have no need to marry. But for those who have not received such a gift, it is better for them to marry than to burn with passion.

Let us not overdraw this matter of virginity. We know Paul was single, but he told Timothy that in the latter times there would be doctrines of demons and of seducing spirits to the effect that marriage would be forbidden (see 1 Tim. 4.1,3). Hence we need to maintain the balance of God's word: we believe on the one hand that virginity and the single life is good, but on the other hand we also believe that marriage is holy too. Marriage has been instituted by God in His very creation from the beginning; and therefore, to forbid to marry is indisputably a doctrine of the demons.

He who does the Lord's work and is already married should so set his family in order that it will be less distracting to his service. Another point to be made here is this: the line between the work and the family must be clear, unless members of one's family are also one's fellow-workers. Otherwise, they should not touch the work or be involved in it. Do not carry the work into the family, nor let your family govern your work. A brother once remarked that he had gone to work for the Lord in a certain place because his wife had made the promise for him! How strange! The fact of the matter is that not only his family, but even his fellow-workers, cannot promise for him. The demarcation between one's family relationship and one's work for God must be sharply delineated. For example, he who serves the Lord must not carelessly tell his family members the spiritual problems of the brothers and sisters in the churches. Members of the family should come to know about these things at the same time as with all other brothers and sisters. Numerous difficulties in the work are created by God's workers talking loosely and indiscriminately to their families.

Still another point to be noticed concerns the proper relationship which must be kept as it pertains to the communication of brothers with sisters and vice versa. If a brother is inclined to work only among the sisters, he should not be allowed to work. Or if a young sister is predisposed to serve primarily among brothers, she should not be permitted to serve. Let us strictly observe the following principle: under normal conditions, brothers should work more among brothers, and sisters more among sisters. The Son of God in the days of His flesh left us with a good example. The line between John 3 and John 4 is very distinctive. In chapter 3 we note that our Lord received Nicodemus at night; in chapter 4 we read that He met the Samaritan woman in broad daylight. According to chapter 3 He most likely received Nicodemus in a house; according to chapter 4 He met the Samaritan woman by a public well. It would have been improper had the environments been reversed so far as the woman was concerned. Our Lord's speaking to Nicodemus and His speaking with the Samaritan woman were under entirely different surroundings. This sets before us a good example to follow.

We are not saying here that there should not be any communication or fellowship between brothers and sisters who are in the work. We would only say that if some brothers and sisters have the disposition of moving about almost exclusively among the opposite sex, then such ones must be stopped. It goes without saying that in Christ there is neither male nor female. There has been no wall set up between brothers and sisters. They should have good fellowship. It is simply wise that for those who have such a nearly exclusive habit of communicating and interacting with the other sex there should be such timely dealing. We hope that brothers and sisters would naturally and spontaneously keep themselves within proper bounds in their interaction with one another. Should anyone overstep beyond the proper limits of fellowship, he or she must be strictly dealt with.

May God be gracious to us that we might bear a good testimony in all these matters. Amen.

TITLES YOU
WILL WANT TO HAVE

by Watchman Nee

Basic Lesson Series
Volume 1—A Living Sacrifice
Volume 2—The Good Confession
Volume 3—Assembling Together
Volume 4—Not I, But Christ
Volume 5—Do All to the Glory of God
Volume 6—Love One Another

The Church and the Work
Volume 1—Assembly Life
Volume 2—Rethinking the Work
Volume 3—Church Affairs

The Character of God's Workman
Gleanings in the Fields of Boaz
The Spirit of the Gospel
The Life That Wins
From Glory to Glory
The Spirit of Judgment
From Faith to Faith
The Lord My Portion
Aids to "Revelation"
Grace for Grace
The Better Covenant
A Balanced Christian Life
The Mystery of Creation
The Messenger of the Cross
Full of Grace and Truth—Volume 1
Full of Grace and Truth—Volume 2
The Spirit of Wisdom and Revelation
Whom Shall I Send?
The Testimony of God
The Salvation of the Soul
The King and the Kingdom of Heaven
The Body of Christ: A Reality
Let Us Pray
God's Plan and the Overcomers
The Glory of His Life
"Come, Lord Jesus"
Practical Issues of This Life
Gospel Dialogue
God's Work
Ye Search the Scriptures
The Prayer Ministry of the Church
Christ the Sum of All Spiritual Things
Spiritual Knowledge
The Latent Power of the Soul
Spiritual Authority
The Ministry of God's Word
Spiritual Reality or Obsession
The Spiritual Man

by Stephen Kaung

Discipled to Christ
The Splendor of His Ways
Seeing the Lord's End in Job
The Songs of Degrees
Meditations on Fifteen Psalms

ORDER FROM:

Christian Fellowship Publishers, inc.
11515 Allecingie Parkway
Richmond, Virginia 23235